I0185784

The Abridged Hodaoa-Anibo Dictionary

Second Edition

Edited by Kobina Wright

Dramatic Pause
Tustin, California

The Abridged Hodaoa-Anibo Dictionary (Second Edition)

Editor: Kobina Wright
Creator: Kobina Wright
Cover Photograph: Copyright 2014

Copyright © 2014
By Dramaticpause Publishing
Tustin, California

ISBN: 978-0975571538

ALL RIGHTS RESERVED
The text in this publication, or any thereof, may not be reproduced or transmitted in any form or by any means, electronic or mechanical including photocopying, recording, storage in an information retrieval system or otherwise without the prior written permission of the publisher.

Printed in the United States of America

Dramatic Pause
P.O. Box 1894
Tustin, CA 92781

"Black people's grace has been with what they do with language."

-Toni Morrison

Table of Contents

Section I

Section II

Introduction

Hodaoa-Anibo, a language created as a work of art, dedicated to the slaves brought to America beginning in 1619, is a controversial and peculiar language. One notable Anibo characteristic is that it does not contain the English translation for the word *fail*. Though the language continues to grow annually in vocabulary, the omission of the word is not an accident.

The etymology of the word from the Merriam-Webster Online Dictionary can be followed from: Middle English *failen,* from Anglo-French *faillir,* from Vulgar Latin *fallire,* alteration of Latin *fallere* to deceive, disappoint. In Anibo, a person cannot fail a test, they cannot fail as a parent or live a life of a failure. In Anibo, the negative connotation is shaved off considerably when something does not happen that is meant, assumed or hoped to have happened. Here a person can do (Henix), or can *not* do (ne Henix), but they can not fail.

Language helps to shape the minds and attitudes and reflect the culture of the people. Two examples. In the 1997 film, Amistad, when the translator, Covey (played by Chiwetel Ejiofor) attempts to translate the word *try* to Cinque (played by Djimon Honsou), he finds that he has a very difficult time of it because in their language and culture, you either do or you don't do. You don't *try*. Although this example is from a movie, it is based on a true event and real issues concerning cultural attitudes driven by language.

Second example: in the Yup'ik Eskimo language there are fifteen different words for *snow*. This fact, of course, demonstrates that snow is an extremely important part of their lives and culture. If the words for snow were absent from Yup'ik Eskimo altogether, it would reflect a polar opposite of their current cultural identity.

Because of the inorganic growth of the Anibo language, and due to the heavy influence of English, for the word *fail* to continue to be absent from Anibo, conscious effort will be required. New words are translated daily through translation of English text, therefore, translation of English speaking attitudes will inadvertently leak into the language as well. Anibo was not created based off of culture but based off of art and history and cannot contain any unique characteristics with out intentional consideration.

Will there be a void without *fail*? Definitely not. Just as there are more words that may not be found in Anibo, likewise, there are words in Anibo that will not be found in English, Spanish, French, Cherokee or Swahili. Similarly, because the grammatical structure is based on Black English Vernacular (African American Vernacular English) there are verb tenses present that cannot be found in Standard American English.

Whether or not the omission of *fail* will have an impact on Anibo speakers cannot be determined now, or any time soon. It will be difficult to measure a shift in attitude or thought until there is a much larger selection of original published Anibo literature or studied dialog. So far there is none. Until then, the mindfulness of its absence can only be noted.

The Alphabet

a – ah	Ħ – sheen	o – o	w - wah
b- bah	i - ee	p – pah	x - iks
d – dah	j – jay	r - rah	y - yot
e – ay	k – kee	s - sun	z - zah
f – fey	l – lay	t - tey	
g – gah	m – mah	u - oo	
h – ha	n – nah	v - vahvey	

Vowel Sounds

The letter "a" in Ħodaoa, makes the same sound as the short
"o" in English.
Example: The "a's" in the word, <u>lawa</u> (meaning *amaze*),
have the same sound as the "o" in <u>mop</u>.

The letter "e" in Ħodaoa, makes a similar sound to the long
"a" in English.
Example: The "e's" in the word, <u>jele</u> (meaning *book*), have
a similar sound to the "a" in <u>pay</u>.

The letter "i" in Ħodaoa, makes the same sound as the long
"e" in English.
Example: The "i" in the word, <u>lami</u> (meaning *animal*), has
the same sound as the "e's" in <u>meet</u>.

The letter "o" in Ħodaoa, makes the same sound as the long
"o" in English.
Example: The "o" in the word, <u>vo</u> (meaning *it*), has the
same sound as the "o" in <u>hope</u>.

The letter "u" in Ħodaoa, makes the same sound as the long
"u" in English.
Example: The letter "u" in the word, <u>upi</u> (meaning *depend*),
has the same sound as the "u" in <u>huge</u>.

Special Rules

1. The "Ħ" – called the "sheen" is pronounced like the "sh" sound in English and is written with two horizontal lines between two vertical lines: Ħ

2. Because there is no symbol on our keyboard for the "sheen," a capital "H" can be used as a substitute in typed text. However to avoid confusion, the "ha" or "h" is NEVER capitalized, even if it is at the beginning of a sentence or begins a person's name.

3. If the letter at the end of the root word is the same letter beginning a suffix, then one of the two letters must be dropped:
   Example: goke (root) + eka (suffix) = gokeka
   (meaning *believed*)

4. To show possession, "ih" is used at the front of a word
   Example: mother's hand = ih'yeye jenu

5. The verb expressing "to be" in present tense is optional similar to Black English Vernacular. This is called the "usual tense."
   Example: John is at the store. = John at the store.

6. The "sd" commonly seen in Ħodaoa – Anibo is pronounced like the "st" sound in English.

7. "-iz" is used instead of "s" to express the plural in words that end in "z," "s," and "j."

8. When expressing future tense using the word "will" and "would" or "umo" and "umon" it is placed at

the end of the verb. Example: "I will walk" would look like "Pa giabumo."

9. The "g" makes the throaty sound of the English "g" in the word "girl" while the "j" is slightly softer than the English "j" sound in the word "jeep."

Numbers

0 none	5 wat	10 deje	30 trewo	80 okawo	400 kadĦ aka
1 pik	6 sis	11 deje pik	40 kadwo	90 nopawo	500 watĦ aka
2 dit	7 sepo	12 deje dit	50 watwo	100 piĦ aka	600 sisĦ aka
3 tre	8 oka	20 diwo	60 siswo	200 ditĦ aka	1000 pikano
4 kad	9 nopa	21 diwo pik	70 sepowo	300 treĦ aka	1,000,000 pik lame

Prefixes

(ab-)	(ko-)
(anti-)	(neno-)
(as-)	(si-)
(auto-)	(fyes-)
(co-)	(ul-)
(con-)	(kis-)
(de-)	(dor-)
(dis-)	(huĦ-)
(inter-)	(nitoe-)
(non-)	(ne-)
(of philosophy or standard)	(jul)
(para-)	(kog-)
(per-)	(gak-)
(possessive)	(ih)
(pre-)	(sde-)
(pro-)	(her-)
(re-)	(Ħo-)
(semi-)	(bem-)
(sub-)	(val-)
(trans-)	(trof-)
(ultra-)	(memi-)
(un-)	(ne-)

Suffixes

('-able)	('-bla)
(-age)	(-jag)
('-al)	(-odi) (-id)
(-an)	(-i)
(-ance)	(-int)
(-ant)	(-ont)
(-ary)	(-aĦe)
(-ate)	(-lj)
(-cy)	(-mla)
(-er)	(-oe)
(-ern)	(-mar)
(-es)	(-iz)
(-est)	(-ba)
(-ette)	(-mle)
(-ful)	(-el)
(future conditional)	(-umon)
(future tense)	(-umo)
(-gress)	(-uĦa)
(-hood)	(-sos)
(-ic)	(-aze)
(-ify)	(-peo)
(infinitive)	(-ekev)
(-ish)	(-aze)
(-ism)	(-zim)
(-ist)	(-izi)
(-ite)	(-ava)
(-ity)	(-une)
(-ive)	(-pugda)
(-ize)	(-lj)
(-less)	(-zne)
(like -y)	(-u)
(-ly)	(-u)
(-ment)	(-bex)
(-ness)	(-wi)
(of philosophy or standard)	(jul)
(of woman)	(-iza)
(-ology)	(-gdata)
(-ory)	(-Ħe)
(-ous)	(-u)
(past tense)	(-eka)
(present –ing)	(-maki)
(-ship)	(-wi)
(-th)	(-u)
(-tion)	(-ekev)
(-try)	(-vik)
(-ty)	(-wi)
(-ure)	(-fte)
(-ute)	(-an)

English Order

A

a	a
a.m.	manlu
abdomen	mimarpo
ability	bleune
able	bla
abort	mlak
abortion	mlakekev
about	gdefda
abroad	faliar
absolute	koukonan
abstract	kolak
abyss	neokaz
accent	azen
accept	honris
accident	kopiem
acclaim	adaoa
accompany	masinbaz
accord	alupıın
according	alupunmaki
account	aliar
ache	akinaga
achieve	laloke
acrobat	akrobat
across	asuazim
act	raka
action	rakekev
active	rakapune
activist	rakapugdaizi
activity	rakapudau
actor	rakoe
actress	rakoi
actual	rakag
actually	rakagu
adapt	kabla
add	mar
addict	kide
addiction	kidekev
addition	marekev
address	ekot
adjust	imri
administer	ulrauoe
admit	maHu
adopt	blum
adoration	ansoekev
adore	anso
advance	motuHa
advantage	agenjag
advertise	kolaklj
advice	maryin
advise	maryin
affect	zimko
affection	zimkoekev
affirm	yeha
after	bulamot
afternoon	bulanopau
afterward	bulamotvo
again	ebu
against	ebuba
age	uros
agent	wutoe
aggressive	zuHu

aggressiveness	zuħuwi
ago	osmidume
agree	agepa
air	blit
airplanes	emer
awkward	dibela
alive	karoron
all	maoe
allegation	legorekev
allege	legor
allow	smeki
almond	lamoz
almost	maumarba
alone	yasmir
along	uveli
already	mawey
alright	ziafe
also	rix
although	tenko
always	maoved
am	sya
amaze	lawa
ambitious	dyaku
American	Ameriki
among	ulin
amount	adaun
amusement	amosbex
analyze	samad
anarchy	agosdi
ancestors	motmabas
and	li
anger	smi
angry	smiu
animal	lami

annual	amemodi
anonymous	namazne
another	ingine
answer	zist
anticipate	omuir
anxiety	axietu
anxious	axiet
any	ma
anyone	mapik
anything	mapgo
apart	akog
apartment	akogbex
apologize	amemlj
apology	amemu
appear	sinit
apple	pum
applesauce	pubaħ
appoint	awega
appointment	awegabex
appreciation	plelin
approach	asilin
approve	osyokum
April	Aneka
arch	bembri
area	lalo
argue	zanenu
argument	zanenubex
arm	haz
armor	umar
around	seonde
arrest	aludlj
arrive	pinkum
arrogant	sipobont
art	ojenis
article	ojeta

artificial	**ga**blu	average	slaxijag
artist	ojeni**si**zi	avoid	apiem
as	aH̵	awake	gdub
ascent	**si**wan	award	**a**blun
aside	**ev**to	aware	**a**er
ask	pal	away	**a**ved
askew	po**da**ma	awe	key
asleep	**ka**yat	axis	**ax**is
aspire	**ka**mo	**B**	
accessories	loir**ku**vip	baby	yunini
associate	ka**we**dlj	bachelor	yadatin
assult	**bil**mla	bachelorette	yadata
assume	**su**mat	back	**bu**lin
assure	**maj**mad	backpack	**bulin**sem
astonish	**la**wa	bad	badz
at	an	badge	**twa**ne
athlete	**sa**kij	bag	**a**jit
athletic	saki**ji**zim	baggy	**aji**tu
attack	reli**no**t	balance	sdij
attend	a**hud**nu	balcony	**ja**konj
attention	ahu**de**kev	ball	nix
attire	**bu**lo	ballad	jum**ye**mu
attitude	**ken**bu	hallot	**na**let
attract	**de**te	banana	banaya
audience	si**koe**	bank	**li**sar
audio	**si**kit	banker	**li**saoe
audition	si**ki**nekev	bar	**wi**dar
August	Kleopa	bare	yek
author	**ro**tu	barely	**ye**ku
authority	ro**tu**ne	base	**yi**mlin
automatic	fyesi**ra**ze	bash	baH̵
automobile	fye**su**ya	basket	**ha**ri
autumn	**da**nil	basketball	**ha**rinix
avail	**a**dyak	bath	wu**be**ta
available	ad**ya**bla	bathroom	H̵iH̵ **ku**lat

battle	**gdo**hint	bile	e**oa**
be	ekev	billion	Ħmi**l**nop
beach	mlar	birth	**web**lem
bead	**bra**ba	birthday	**web**lem-**sdu**me
bear	pla**ve**ji	bitter	**ja**gda
beat	**mle**ub	black	**ye**po
beautiful	me**kae**l	blame	**lan**uj
beauty	me**ka**	blank	**sde**li
because	**ev**pedonj	bleat	blit
become	ev**rel**in	bleed	duleka
bed	**gde**ga	blemish	donaze
bedroom	gdega **ku**lat	blend	mlan
been	ekev**eka**	bless	dej
beer	bir	blind	**tre**Hi
before	sde**po**mot	blink	**afa**
befriend	evĦevun	bliss	**a**mej
beg	mla**da**	blister	man**oe**
begin	roko**zu**ja	blond	**kar**tavi
behavior	eke**vg**da	blood	dul
behind	**bu**la	bloodthirsty	dulgdan**kau**
belief	**go**ket	bloom	blum
believe	**go**ke	blossom	**zou**ti
bend	trat	blouse	blos
benefit	at**u**ot	blow	**wa**bo
beneficial	at**u**otlj	blue	luk
beside	**ev**to	blur	mlur
best	**an**ba	board	buk
bet	gef	boast	**tra**o
better	**a**ne	body	**ker**po
between	evu**H**	bomb	**zo**lum
beyond	eke**n**izuj	book	**je**le
bicep	**di**fit	boost	tre**lua**
bicycle	di**onde**	booth	**fu**am
bid	**ha**fla	border	atoe
big	faĦabaz	bore	**tre**vo

bored	trevoeka	brush	pat**av**ye
born	weblem**e**ka	brut	yuk
borrow	**mo**ma	brutal	yuk**o**di
boss	sdew**oe**	bucket	**zi**ki
both	**ha**mi	buff	buf
bother	bod	build	mlo
bottom	**bi**po	building	mloH̵
box	**xa**bo	bully	yuk
boxers	xab**oes**	bunch	**to**bes
boy	om**aj**	burgundy	**mog**dul
boyfriend	om**aj**H̵evun	burn	**mog**da
bra	**dab**dar	business	alk**ina**wi
brag	**tra**o	busy	**al**ko
braid	**plo**ka	but	zan
branch	**pat**rin	butt	ezin**se**
brand	**pat**ri	button	**fa**rem
brass	mlat	buy	**ber**a
brave	sde**pe**bla	by	**ya**su
break	**ax**e	**C**	
breakfast	mal**o**ji	cable	**tye**v
breast	**da**bej	café	**ka**fe
breath	blun	calendar	uba**me**moe
breed	**ka**bos	call	**un**e
breeze	abaz	callous	**bo**vu
bride	**gue**su	calm	paz
brief	ja**jo**e	camera	**twil**sir
briefcase	jajoetot	camp	xix
bright	**sdo**na	campaign	xix**an**e
bring	**gde**fe	can	ra
broad	**gu**bir	candid	**zo**wan
broom	**ba**rum	candidacy	zowanljune
brother	**ki**po	candidate	zow**anl**j
brow	**ta**vey	cannot	**ra**ne
brown	**bo**ron	canvas	**pu**gun
bruise	ata	cap	saf

cappuccino	kapu**Ħ**ino	character	azgaoe
capture	**saf**te	charge	**tine**
car	ka**ve**hi	charisma	mun**za**wa
card	**ru**bri	charismatic	mun**za**ze
care	brak	charm	**ulan**
career	la**koz**	chat	Ħat
carry	**be**ok	chatter	Ħatoe
cartoon	ka**tun**	cheap	sler
carve	**ho**yi	check	**pla**kli
case	tot	checkpoint	plakie**we**ga
cast	**wo**ne	cheek	keĦ
cat	sok	chest	**bi**not
catch	a**fu**la	chic	nik
category	kati**r**gu	child	**az**yej
catwalk	sok**gi**ab	childhood	**az**yej**s**os
cause	**ped**onj	children	**az**ye**j**iz
caution	brak	chill	**ok**Ħun
cautionary	braka**Ħe**	choice	tu**az**ing
cautious	**brak**u	choke	Ħok
ceiling	uta**ma**ki	choose	tu**az**ib
celebrate	**tri**nilj	Christmas	Aze**ji**mi
celebrity	tri**nu**ne	chronicle	**ne**mi
cell phone	**sel**is	chuckle	hi**Ħ**ni
cent	**a**kat	chunk	ki**pe**kev
center	mid**oe**	church	kani**m**la
central	mid**o**di	churn	atili
century	a**ka**fe	cigar	**si**ka
certain	sun	cigarette	**si**ka**m**le
certainty	sunune	circle	**on**de
chain	von	circulate	**on**delj
chair	bi**pa**ri	citizen	sitioe
challenge	**hu**luj	city	**si**ti
chance	**me**Ħun	civil	sia**Ħ**a
change	meĦomi	claim	daoa
channel	Ħano	clap	klap

clarity	Hiegune	comedy	plamla
clasp	mima	comfort	sinmo
class	klato	comforter	sinmoe
clay	sdemlepo	comic	plaze
clean	Hi	comment	sinbex
clear	Hiego	commercial	sinodi
clearest	Hiegoba	commit	sinli
clerk	kera	commitment	sinlibex
client	mlebo	committee	sinlioe
clientele	mlebo	commune	sina
climate	klilj	communism	sinazim
climb	mazaz	communist	sinaizi
cling	artir	community	sinapik
clip	octa	compact	sinsem
close	serad	companion	sinlao
cloth	lo	company	sinabaz
clothes	lonkas	compare	rele
cloud	klo	compass	relun
clown	pagakon	compassion	relunekev
clue	kijin	compete	sinum
coach	kari	complain	sinkonka
coat	kot	complex	sinplex
cobalt	kobalt	complicate	sinplelj
code	hitib	computer	siney
coffee	yepanj	concept	kisfit
cold	okH	concern	kiskaet
colleague	kolaga	conclude	kisfluj
collect	kundi	confer	kisnoe
collection	dundiekev	confess	kisaH
college	kolej	confidence	kisnint
colonial	blonodi	confidante	kisnont
color	pimey	confide	kisnix
comb	mleke	confirm	kisfluey
come	relin	conflict	kisetot
comedian	plamlai	confuse	nefu

English		English	
congress	kongres	count	ubam
conjure	ulap	counter	ubamoe
connect	uhev	country	oduar
conscious	kispitwu	couple	ditana
consensus	kisnajinu	courage	sdepebla
conservative	kisrenpugda	course	mlenj
consider	kisratlj	court	kort
consist	kiseyu	cousin	etaki
conspicuous	uamu	cover	gdiln
conspirator	kisHibioe	cow	zabi
conspire	kisHibi	cowboy	zabiomaj
consult	marinub	crack	krak
consultant	marinubont	cradle	sagar
contain	serket	crash	kaz
contest	kisflungo	crawl	relao
context	kisjebix	crazy	haka
continue	miladit	create	azye
contribute	kisbrajma	creativity	azyekevu
contribution	kisbrajmaekev	credential	gokovont
conundrum	ribix	credibility	gokovwi
convene	kisin	credible	gokoble
convention	kisinekev	credit	afoti
convert	kisHomi	credit	gokovo
cookie	fula	crew	gorupem
cool	kul	crime	yevla
copy	pleit	critic	gina
cord	lupun	critical	ginaodi
corner	ganom	cross	suaz
correct	wafe	crowd	gakubaz
correction	wafekev	crusade	yawelj
corrupt	mlagan	cry	zigu
cost	xali	culture	kufte
cotton	koton	cup	kombe
could	muyaye	curious	sduziju
council	marinoe	curse	majix

curtain	rutuk	deject	dorlaHi
curve	loroi	delegate	ukazolj
cut	Hrep	delude	doryofe
cute	mleHuni	delusion	doryofeykev
cycle	onde	demand	lesin
D		demise	doroklj
daily	sdumu	democracy	demokramla
damage	Hapodit	democratic	demokraze
dance	bajun	demonstrate	sdejalj
danger	blulir	denounce	huHyokem
dangerous	bluliru	deny	dorne
dare	guak	depend	upi
dark	Hij	depress	dorlaHi
date	Hemi	depression	dorlaHiekev
daughter	jeki	deputy	proHi
day	sdume	descent	dorwan
deal	gapit	desert	uwabe
death	okazo	design	ziwio
debacle	slu-pleme	designer	ziwioe
debated	debu	desire	nopote
decade	dejede	destiny	lamejul
December	Nandi	detail	dorejag
decide	biHoket	detain	dorepoɑ
decision	biHoketev	detract	dorlak
declare	medoj	develop	aswakau
décor	huHpi	devoid	ledwamaki
decorate	huHpilj	diamond	sdajlun
decrease	dormarek	dictate	yof
dedicate	twotlj	dictator	yofoe
deed	yum	dictionary	sdepevmla
deep	liamu	die	xfar
define	dorbal	diet	diet
definition	dorbalekev	different	zaneli
deflect	dorum	difficult	zahubri
degree	ealu	dinner	samoj

dinning room	**kor**on **kul**at
dip	dip
diploma	labo**kaz**o
diplomacy	labok**ekev**
direct	wan
direction	wan**ekev**
dirt	**vig**da
disagree	huⱧa**gep**a
disappear	huⱧ**s**init
disappointment	huⱧ**a**weg
discourage	huⱧsde**pebla**
discover	sen**ul**a
discrete	ser**ip**i
disgrace	huⱧ**tuf**a
disgust	huⱧ**fa**blu
disk	**ud**e
dislike	ne**lik**a
displace	huⱧyem
dissent	huⱧa**gep**a
dissenter	huⱧa**gep**a**oe**
dissident	huⱧa**gep**a**oe**
distance	**log**int
distant	**log**ont
distinct	**log**a
distinctive	lo**gaze**
distract	**huH**lak
distraught	vi**huH**yuj
disturb	e**fel**e
dive	dip
divide	**bla**min
do	Ⱨenix
documentary	wu**kat**ij
dodge	gaj
dog	nao**le**
dollar	**zap**i

dominance	**tin**int
done	Ⱨeniye
door	**wul**a
doorman	wula**maje**
doorstep	la**dia**
dot	dat
doubt	**uf**an
down	slu
downtown	slut**one**
dozen	a**go**ja
drag	**vur**po
drama	**ongy**ar
dramatic	o**ngya**ru
draw	mlif
dream	gdar
dress	**bul**o
dress (n)	**ze**jup
drift	**a**sey
drink	**fu**a
drip	**dit**e
drive	**sdak**i
drop	hap
drop	**dif**u
drug	**po**dint
drum	dek
dry	linj
dub	ha
duo	**dit**u
during	flonu**mak**i
duty	**ea**z
dynamic	**wa**bip

E

each	int
eager	est
eagerness	**est**wi

ear	**mi**sa	end	o**ka**zo
early	**bu**lat	endless	neokaz
Earth	Art	endure	**ro**nur
earth	**vi**gda	enemy	gabuba
east	maHarij	energetic	ene**je**du
easy	**mla**ba	energize	ene**je**dlj
eat	**ko**ron	energy	ene**je**dip
echo	**da**fu	enforce	en**mo**tega
economy	ve**ni**bya	enforcement	en**mo**tegabex
ecstatic	ba**le**do	English	**In**gleH
edge	**o**kar	enjoy	niHua
edit	loj	enough	**fli**ni
editor	lo**jo**e	enter	**ni**toe
editorial	lo**jo**di	entertain	**ni**topa
educate	pe**do**kalj	enthusiasm	ma**o**zim
educated	pe**do**kal**je**ka	enthusiastic	mao**a**ze
education	pe**do**ka**e**kev	envelop	swa**ka**u
effort	**au**ban	envelope	swa**ka**u
eighth	o**ka**u	environment	ve**ni**bex
either	riH	envision	wu**e**kev
elaborate	**nui**dorlj	equal	u**ku**a
elbow	**je**te	equality	u**ku**ne
elect	**gi**la	erupt	**ru**fer
election	**gi**la**e**kev	escape	e**sa**y
elite	**sli**li	essay	**sa**ni
else	**ma**ra	establish	ya**po**naze
email	e**ka**gix	establishment	ya**po**na**ze**bex
embarrass	ne**o**ta	esteem	u**wo**dar
embrace	**mlu**	estimate	hi**nu**ba
emerge	o**ayn**	estimation	hi**nu**bekev
emergency	o**ayn**imla	ethnic	**ha**vlu
emphasis	**im**fas	ethnicity	hav**lu**ne
empty	**am**tip	Europe	U**ro**pe
encounter	ni**tu**bamoe	European	U**ro**pi
encounter	ni**bam**oe	even	**a**ga

eventual	agatuodi
ever	eki
every	ekiu
everyone	ekiupik
evil	okor
evolve	ekond
exact	xaka
exactly	xakau
example	roaba
exchange	bluti
excite	ruyava
excuse	imon
executive	beosapugda
exercise	labin
exist	ekev
expand	sdas
expatriate	xpatriat
expect	omuir
expense	xali
experience	osmad
expert	yogoe
expiration	impirekev
expire	impir
explain	yikonka
explicit	implaka
explode	implawabip
exploit	imlakari
exploration	implakiekev
explore	implaki
explosive	implawapugda
expose	xine
express	yelada
extra	zeme
extraordinary	zemazi
eye	uan

F

fabricate	haditilj
fabrication	haditiekev
face	pabo
fact	sdiki
factor	sdikiℍe
factory	sdikiℍeu
faith	trajin
fake	gablu
fall (n)	danil
fall (v)	pleme
fame	aje
familiar	ajegir
family	ajega
famous	ajeu
fan	jab
fanatic	ejenata
fancy	ejeplik
fantasy	ejenamla
far	faline
fascinate	zugoklj
fashion	gadine
fast	gada
fat	belole
father	bati
faux	gablu
favor	gini
favorite	giniba
fax	didni
fear	vip
feature	yoniln
February	hatℍe
federal	fedodi
feed	gam
feel	dum

feet	**pa**mans	flow	Hugomey
female	fe**nu**ma	flowers	**ga**wars
feminine	fe**nu**maze	fluff	flaf
feminism	fe**numz**im	fluffy	**fla**fu
feminist	fe**nu**mizi	flutter	flit
few	aler	fly	**ba**ig
fiction	gdie**kev**	focus	**fo**dor
fifth	**wa**tu	fold	donada
fight	**fu**ba	folklore	gaku**kau**
figure	**sman**ki	follow	**ple**ta
fill	eli	following	**ple**tamaki
film	**hi**gu	food	koj**me**de
final	**blen**up	fool	slas
finale	**blen**up	foot	**pa**man
finance	**ku**nint	footage	pama**jag**
find	**pe**tu	for	mot
fine	bal	forbid	**mo**fla
finger	**ho**naj	force	motega
finish	Heniye	forefathers	motbabas
fire	a**jo**te	forehead	mo**ken**in
firm	**flu**ey	foreign	**ni**zuj
first	o**zu**ja	foreigner	nizujoe
fish	nag	forever	moteki
fit	oim	forge	**mo**tip
fix	**ba**bri	forget	motupun
fixate	**ba**brilj	forgive	motejma
fixation	babrilje**kev**	form	**go**bet
flag	**pla**set	formal	gobetodi
flamboyance	kodi**ku**dint	format	gogobeta
flamboyant	kodi**ku**dont	former	gobetoe
flame	**ma**fle	fortune	motale
flat	**ta**hak	forward	motuHa
flight	bai**gava**	found	petueka
float	**va**fa	foundation	petuekaekev
floor	gdu	fourth	**ka**du

France	Frans	gender	**de**ra
franchise	**pa**trinlj	gene	**der**ney
fraud	**ga**bos	general	loima
freak	**ro**ding	generation	der**ekev**
free	van**au**	genetic	de**raze**
freedom	vanau**sos**	gentle	**gum**la
French	Frenℍ	genuine	**a**is
frenzy	**her**po	get	**du**pun
frequency	vami**ont**mla	ghost	gos
frequent	vam**iont**	giant	dofaℍont
fresh	**wa**ka	gift	ej**i**mi
Friday	Ju**pis**dum	gin	gin
friend (plus)	ye**kle**vun	ginger	gin**goe**
friends	ℍevuns	girl	oj**u**ma
friendship	ℍe**vun**wi	give	**ej**ma
from	sko	glare	**plo**ha
front	**sde**po	glass	**xi**ni
frown	**ja**ni	glide	akwetlu
fulfill	el**i**li	global	seo**ko**di
full	**el**i	globe	seo**ko**
fumble	**fe**mu	go	mip
fun	plaℍ	God	**A**za
function	kapu**ekev**	gold	smup
fund	**di**ya	gone	mip**ek**a
further	fal**inoe**	good	**gi**ye
fuse	**tra**ni	goodbye	**se**paz
future	eko	goose bump	**sa**san
fuzz	fuz	got	dupu**nek**a
G		govern	**go**vu
gain	mlaf	government	go**vu**bex
game	**ga**ri	governor	govu**oe**
garage	ka**ve**hi **ku**lat	grab	**gde**da
gasped	**mu**kif	grace	**tu**fa
gather	**kun**di	graffiti	itefa**ni**ti
gaze	**yi**mey	grain	fent

grainy	**fen**tu	hallucinate	ha**sova**jlj
grand	**ku**ja	hallucination	ha**sova**jekev
grandfather	kuja**bati**	hammer	de**foe**
grandmother	kuja**yeye**	hand	**je**nu
grant	**ja**zad	handful	**je**nuel
grapefruit	re**fuit**	handicap	ezu**toe**
graph	itef	handsome	hanᚻuni
gravitate	mliflj	hang	**ha**vi
gravity	mli**fava**	haphazard	bem**le**pli
great	**le**fij	happen	twak
greed	**lav**mar	happy	**yu**ja
greedy	lav**ma**ru	hard	**hu**bri
green	**mun**je	harassed	huneᚻemo
greeting	**se**paz	harsh	hask
grey	**gu**ay	has	**si**gda
groove	e**vo**ri	hat	**ken**flej
grotesque	bav**yi**ka	hate	zow
ground	ding	have	**si**gda
group	**vad**ni	hazard	**le**pli
grow	**bi**dar	he	**en**ey
guarantee	kla**sa**fu	head	**ken**in
guard	**kis**pir	heal	ferᚻ
guess	**hi**ni	health	**fer**ᚻu
guest	**ne**pu	hear	sdis
guide	nun	heart	**sde**plet
guitar	**gi**tar	heartfelt	**sde**pletdumek
gun	bix	heat	**ho**vi
gusto	**fa**blu	heave	**lu**tum
gymnasium	jem	heavy	**lu**tumu
H		heel	fe**dua**
habit	ᚻo**go**pu	height	**si**pa
habitat	ᚻo**go**puan	heir	**sa**ga
habitually	ᚻo**go**podiu	helicopter	**ta**zot
hair	ta**vi**mir	hell	ra**bu**deg
half	bem	hello	**se**paz

help	**gdo**me	house	so**sango**
help	sag	how	spleyn
her	**ih**'enin	however	zan
here	**ga**zu	hug	mlu
heritage	nisag**vo**jag	huge	ki
hey	ey	human	pi**ma**je
hide	**hi**tem	humanity	pima**je**pik
hierarch	sa**gam**bri	humble	**pim**ble
hierarchy	sa**gam**briu	humor	pla**Ħ**u
high	sip	hunger	**la**vat
highway	**si**ved	hungry	**la**vatu
hinder	bu**no**e	hurt	e**gim**
hint	hent	husband	**nab**su
hip	**le**muk	hush	**Ħ**u**Ħ**
hip	ley		
hire	**el**sip	**I**	
his	**ih**'eney	ice	raf
hispanic	his**pa**ni	idea	**pa**lit
hiss	**Ħ**es	ideal	pa**li**jul
history	hadi**Ħ**e	identification	bahue**kev**
hit	**o**te	identify	ba**hu**klu
hold	**az**nu	if	ix
home	**Ħ**ome	ignite	wa**la**va
honey	**eye**ra	ignorant	ne**Ħ**osoe
honor	**bra**ta	ignore	ne**Ħ**os
hope	**fla**ya	ikon	kap
hopeful	fla**ya**el	illuminate	bu**jir**lj
horrible	**Ħe**okble	illuminous	bu**ji**nu
horror	**Ħe**ok	illustrate	bu**jet**lj
horse	**ha**tav	illustration	bu**je**kev
hospital	**Ħe**wigag	image	**ni**ja
host	to**po**e	imagination	nijapeo**ekev**
hostage	ya**su**jag	imagine	nija**pe**o
hot	jotz	immediate	**kis**velj
hour	**o**re	immediately	**kis**velj
		immigrant	niza**i**zi

immigration	nizaekev	inhabitant	niHogopuan
immoral	mlagan	inherent	nisagont
immune	jey	inherit	nisagvo
immortal	belifid	injustice	nipinifu
immortalize	belifidlj	inmate	nijefa
impenetrable	niferabla	inner-city	nisiti
imperialism	imperiodizim	innocent	nisoHis
implicate	uleyulj	inquire	bersi
imply	uleyu	inseparable	nehuHplabla
import	nidari	inside	nito
important	nidariont	insist	nizi
impossible	neHenabla	insomnia	nesomnea
impress	ulseta	inspiration	enimusekev
impression	ulsetaekev	inspire	enimuse
improvement	anebex	instead	nisdene
in	ni	instinct	nipeki
inauguration	nidiabekev	institute	ableyem
inch	flir	institution	ableyemekev
include	nifluj	instruct	flionde
income	nirelin	instruction	fliondedev
incorporate	mlokazu	integrate	nitojin
increase	nimarek	intellect	dazeko
incredible	nigokabla	intellectual	dazekolj
Indeed	niyum	intelligent	dazekond
independent	niupiekev	intend	ninin
indigenous	kerkoze	intense	nibapi
individual	niblamiodi	intent	ninin
induce	niklu	intention	ninekev
industry	zofivik	interracial	nitoeyolejodi
inevitable	nitwabla	intercept	nitoeHok
inflamed	niseyeka	interest	kaet
inflect	nerum	internal	nitoenodi
inform	nigobet	international	nitoeyunanod
information	nigobetekev	international	nitoyunodi
infuse	nitrani	intimate	niponilj

intimidate	nitabelj	journalist	juiteba
into	nika	journey	jutavu
introduce	nitoeklu	joy	Hua
intrude	axni	judge	ujot
intruder	axnioe	judgment	ujotbex
invade	nirev	juice	ekiwa
invest	taletiem	July	haniba
investigate	taletizoula	jump	rub
investigation	taletizoulev	June	Makeda
investment	taletiembex	junk	gdaye
invite	nihava	just	pini
invoke	nifine	justice	pinifu
involve	niekond		

K

iron	iron	keep	pepo
is	sya	keep	zir
isolated	apikya	key	gavi
issue	vasapu	kick	kik
it	vo	kidnap	rablem
Italian	Italin	kill	zaga
Italy	Italu	kind	syen
itch	plinit	kiss	yol
item	piad	kitchen	gdunuj
itself	vomirum	knee	oajde
		know	yoket
		known	yoketumon

J

L

jacket	janit	labor	labo
jail	fiaj	lack	ledwa
January	lmho	lady	serum
jaunt	jufa	lake	oapa
jean	jin	land	lapa
jewelry	yepeko	language	mliajag
jingle	ableyem	large	faHabaz
job	spim	lash	taveH
join	yelao	last	okazing
joke	plaHlj		
journal	junal		

late	**sda**fe	light	**imya**
later	**sda**foe	lightening	sda**ja**faH
laugh	**pa**ga	like	**li**ka
law	laj	likewise	**li**ka**dada**
law	kli	line	**ba**nil
lawn	**la**ri	link	**le**ti
lawyer	kli**oe**	lip	**hi**jes
lay	**na**i	list	skap
lead	**sdep**go	listen	si**ki**lan
leader	sdep**goe**	literature	a**zif**te
leadership	sdep**gowi**	little	mle
leap	ku	live (n)	**ro**ron
learn	**sdu**at	live (v)	**ro**ko
least	e**bar**ba	liver	**mer**mi
leave	mi**line**	living room	**ro**ko **ku**lat
left (direction)	**sa**bom	loath	**ma**ve
leg	**nue**	local	**nye**ji
legal	la**jo**di	locate	nyelj
legend	ra**lo**san	lock	**and**ye
lemon	**su**ert	lodge	plap
lemonade	**su**er**ta**to	logo	**he**su
less	**baz**ne	long	**nu**ir
lesson	**az**ni	look	**sa**ma
let	**sme**ki	loose	**a**be
letter	**be**ga	lord	vlun
level	uH	lose	**pi**su
liaison	ye**la**gau	loss	**pi**Hu
lib	**da**te	lost	pisu**e**ka
liberal	**da**teodi	lot	**ha**ra
liberate	**da**telj	loud	e**da**mik
lick	**la**me	loudly	e**da**moku
lie	snuj	love	**ye**je
life	ro**ko**ze	low	slu
lifestyle	ro**ko**zesma	lower	slu**oe**
lift	**hi**mon	luck	me**H**un

lull	ako	match	**a**mo**t**u
lullaby	ako**m**i	material	ira**s**odi
lunch	**go**ro	mathematic	ama**j**ukint
lure	lur	matron	matron
lust	**kam**ma	matter	**ira**s
luxury	**mir**ko	mattress	taha**k**as

M

machine	ma**k**i**ne**	maven	yo**goe**
magazine	**ma**gaz	maximum	**me**milj
mail	**ka**gix	May (month)	**Ne**fer
main	fya	may	**sa**man
mainstream	fya**sas**da	maybe	sa**manev**
maintain	fye**po**a	me	pa
major	**ska**jav	meal	**po**ji
majority	skaja**vu**ne	mean	**ba**ni
make	klu	measure	**ma**ko
male	si**maj**	medal	**de**muk
man	**ma**je	media	**yo**in
manage	**ma**jeg	meet	**mi**nom
manners	uma**doe**	memoir	katije
manpower	majeye**oe**	memory	**ka**te
manufacture	fas**dif**te	mention	sdi**ga**go
many	**fa**baz	merge	ayn
map	**ram**ni	merit	**me**re
march	mar**н**	mess	**po**di
March	**Tiye**	message	itenu
marines	ma**ri**nes	metabolism	meta**bo**zim
mark	**do**in	method	**au**dix
market	blir	methodic	audix**aze**
marriage	**plong**jag	methodically	**au**dixazeu
marry	plong	middle	mid
martyr	martr	might	**po**gda
mass	flum	mighty	po**gda**u
massive	flum**pu**gda	migrate	za
masterpiece	lefibo	mild	**da**ka
		mile	**mi**le

military	xa
milk	maH
milkshake	maHjote
mind	nin
mine	ih'pas
mine (n)	ben
miniskirt	plismla
minister	rauoe
minor	fen
minority	fenune
minute	fey
mirror	lamirj
miserable	ramabla
misery	ramaga
miss	dyen
mission	fodix
mix	ato
mobile	uya
model	tux
moderate	dernlj
modern	dernu
moist	oato
moisture	oafte
mold (for copy)	tenix
mold (fungus)	toaba
moment	Haye
Monday	Lunsdum
money	diya
monsters	rodoe
month	anda
moon	lune
more	mara
morning	manlu
most	marba
mother	yeye

motivate	avedo
motivation	avedoekev
mount	uhev
mouth	unipi
move	godo
movement	godobex
movie	goyelun
much	fama
mud	gada
mumble	sileble
murder	zaga
music	jeyele
must	sike
myself	pamirum
mystery	pauli

N

nail	gakay
naïve	neyokma
naked	unelo
name	nama
nap	yet
narrative	wabe
nation	yunan
national	yunanodi
nationality	yunanodiune
native	nativ
nature	soeHen
navel	levij
near	paHedo
need	uhitaka
negative	nesyea
neighbor	togar
neighborhood	togarsos
neither	neriH
nerve	tramlit

never	neĦi	oblique	valĦijwi
new	rokip	observe	uawa
newcomer	yokiplindoe	obsess	kiduĦ
newsletter	rokibega	obstacles	blaboz
newspaper	yokipseran	obtain	pepoa
next	garline	obvious	uamu
nice	tus	occupy	magun
nickname	Ħognama	occur	ram
night	beslum	occurrence	ramint
ninth	nopau	ocean	leji
no	ne	October	Musa
no one	nepik	odd	bunup
nobody	nepik	of	bari
nod	palat	off	dibey
nominate	samwlj	offend	dibazo
nominee	samwa	offense	dibajag
none	sedo	offensive	dibazpugda
nonpartisan	nekogaze	offer	dajir
noon	nopau	office	yaletaflo
nor	nefa	official	yabetaflodi
north	askanij	often	gota
nose	virgda	oil	zenk
note	itenu	okay	zafe
nothing	neapgo	old	fanin
notice	itenu	on	ladit
notary	iteĦanu	once	piĦki
novel	rokiĦe	only	genu
novelist	rokiĦizi	open	zoula
November	Zinga	opera	arik
now	Ħaron	opinion	ari
nudity	ulnelowi	opportunity	jirond
number	Ħuba	optimism	wuekevizim

O

		option	wumaekev
oar	owars	or	fa
object	obya	orange	ronj

order	dunu	paranoia	dismilit
ordinary	dunaHe	paranoid	dismilitoe
organization	syenljekev	parent	koganis
organize	syenlj	park	poak
origin	kera	parking	poakmaki
original	kerkaodi	part	kog
orphan	faosmej	particle	koeodi
orphanage	faosmiejag	particular	kogekili
other	siga	partner	yelo
otherwise	sigakada	party	kogaHe
ounce	onz	pass	osmidum
our	ih'jas	passion	gden
out	nine	passive	osmipugda
outrage	zovurous	passport	osmidum
outside	nineto	past (time)	osmidueka
over	loir	pastor	kanimla kenir
overwhelm	loirtrevo	path	hale
own	gen	patience	dint

P

		patriotism	patriotzim
p.m.	valu	pay	slati
pace	pahagdin	pea	pea
pack	sem	peace	sepaz
package	semjag	peach	kalsesi
page	gagun	pedigree	pedigri
pain	amatwa	peek	delinj
paint	hapimey	pen	xomla
painting (n)	hapojen	pencil	xovi
pair	ditana	penetrate	feralj
pajamas	ajami	penis	bafeni
palpable	uamu	pepper	epli
panties	jajikis	perceive	mikefin
pants (n)	jajis	percent	doaka
paper	eran	perception	mikefinekev
parade	diato	perfect	gakau
parallel	lamoluj	perfection	gakauekev

perhaps	ga**ku**twa	pleat	loada
perk	mler**H**	plight	sub
permission	pri**ma**son	plum	ye**pu**li
persist	ga**ki**zi	poem	**ni**bo
person	**ga**kup	poet	ni**bo**e
personal	gaku**po**di	poetry	ni**bo**vik
personality	gaku**po**dune	point	e**we**ga
personally	gaku**po**diu	police	poli**so**e
persuade	anvu**H**ato	policy	**kua**
perturb	iri**bl**a	polish	hey
petal	ativ**l**u	polish	zey
phantom	e**j**enti	polite	tu**sa**va
photo	**twi**li	politic	kua**zim**
photograph	twil**it**ef	political	kua**zim**odi
photographer	twilite**fo**e	poll	pol
pick	**H**ir	polygamist	pole**ga**mu
pick	**sk**iwi	polygamy	pole**ga**mu
picture	**ye**lun	poor	yi
piece	**di**po	porn	**ze**gi
pillow	**o**er	pornographic	**ze**giyeluna**ze**
place	yem	port	**da**ri
plagiarism	edi**ko**zim	portion	doke**kev**
plagiarist	edi**ko**izi	portray	**da**sda
plaid	plad	pose	**fo**sa
plain	**kon**ka	position	fose**kev**
plan	**sa**wa	positive	fos**ye**a
planets	**yo**cup	possess	**si**gda
plant	**sa**wan	possible	fos**yi**ble
plate	bai**bin**	posture	fosa**kef**te
platform	tan**go**bet	potential	hub**lo**di
play	**gdu**hi	pour	**yi**bla
player	gduhi**o**e	powder	po**vo**da
playwright	gdu**hi**te	power	**ye**oe
please	yi**o**pa	powerful	**ye**oel
pleasure	ye**o**bex	practical	vika**ze**odi

practice	vik	privilege	tavujag
pray	ebri	prize	danHa
prayer	ebrioe	probable	hernoble
preach	brint	probably	hernoblu
precise	anwega	probe	herno
precision	anwekev	problem	herdon
prefer	sdedi	process	seHi
preference	sdeditint	produce	herklu
pregnant	ulaz	product	herki
premier	sdemirj	profess	heraH
premise	sduan	professor	heraHoe
preparatory	sdegdaHe	profound	herpetek
prepare	sdegda	program	herip
present	gakukazo	progress	heruHa
preside	gdim	progressive	heruHaekev
presidency	gdimoemla	project	herHi
president	gdimoe	prominent	biyoketont
press	laHiseta	promise	dal
pressure	laHisetalj	promote	herave
prestige	eyaf	prop	seloe
prestigious	eyafu	proper	seloe
pretend	sdefe	property	selewi
pretty	reti	protagonist	herazizi
price	xali	protection	herspiekev
pride	gelen	protest	kwanuri
primary	ozaHe	prototypical	hersyenodi
prime	ozuja	proud	gele
prince	ajum	prove	syokum
princess	ajumiza	provide	hermin
principle	ajujul	psych	syeki
print	iteslu	psyche	syekiu
priority	tamle	public	pluaze
prison	Hofai	publicity	pluatune
privacy	tavumla	publish	klupluaz
private	tavulj	pull	tamya

English		English	
pump	Hugomey	reality	dindipau
purse	sajit	realize	dindlj
pursuit	Has	really	dindu
push	rade	reason	Hoad
put	swey	recall	Houne
Q		receive	Hofi
quadriceps	kadefi	recent	Hobreit
qualified	dyupeo	recent	zensen
quality	dyune	recently	zensenu
quest	domax	receptive	Hofipugda
question	domaxev	recess	HoduH
quick	gada	recline	bimai
quiet	twama	recognition	rekonat
quit	vagHi	record	Hozir
R		recover	Hogdiln
race	yolej	rectangle	lakat
racial	yolejodi	red	saka
racism	yolejzim	reduce	Hoklu
radio	radio	refer	Hobradit
rage	vuros	reflect	Horum
rain	doklo	reflection	Horumekev
rainbow	doklo-bembri	reform	Hogobet
raise	bis	refuse	HoneHen
rank	tamya	regain	Homlaf
rare	ejpo	regard	Hokispir
rather	roved	regimen	zikisak
rattle	hanlo	reject	HoHi
rave	memika	rejection	HoHiekev
reach	rint	relate	Hodokat
react	Horaka	relationship	Hodokevwi
reaction	Horakekev	relative	Hodokapugda
read	lum	relax	Hona
ready	tyari	religion	Hotrima
reaffirm	Hoyeha	reluctant	wadin
real	dind	remark	Hodoin

remarkable	Hodoinabla	retail	Hotal
remember	Hokate	retain	Hoepoa
remind	Honin	retract	Holak
remit	HoaH	retrieve	goveHiumo
remove	Hogodo	return	Hosupine
renew	Hoyokip	reveal	digowe
renown	ajeu	revise	gowu
rent	utwaj	revision	gowuekev
repeat	gopetum	revolution	Hoekonekev
replace	Hoyem	revolutionary	Hoekonekevu
report	Hodar	revolve	Hoekond
reporter	Hodaroe	reward	Hoejma
represent	Hogakukazo	rewarding	Hoejmaki
representative	Hogakukazoe	rhetoric	neziaze
repress	HolaHi	rhetorically	neziazu
republic	Hopluaze	rich	iey
reputation	Horekev	riddle	ribix
repute	Hora	ride	gaHote
require	Hopal	ridiculous	rixahu
rescue	Hoefe	rifle	refiles
research	Hojonu	right	wafe
resent	Hosin	right (direction)	sahop
resentful	Hosinel	righteous	watrefe
reside	Hoto	ring	bri
residence	Hotoebex	rip	sikuala
resident	Hotoe	rise	brisa
resign	Hogiwi	risk	enata
resignation	Hogiwinekev	river	oag
respect	Hogek	road	liar
respond	Hosdeli	roar	woha
response	Hodeis	rock	pya
responsible	Hosdeble	rocket	pyaka
rest	ludu	rod	rod
restaurants	koronis	role	apue
restore	Homri	roll	lol

romance	amorint	scene	**pa**li
roof	uf	schedule	nu**a**fue
room	**ku**lat	school	esko**m**la
root	rut	science	val**tri**ma
round	**on**de	score	twir
routine	**lo**lir	scout	fos**ki**lan
rug	**gdi**ka	scratch	slan
rule	**ku**a	screen	**ha**bo
run	**a**sli	script	**sa**rip
rush	**sde**mu	seal	**u**ta
rust	**he**to	sear	sir

S

		search	**jo**nu
sacrifice	taЋomi	season	ni**ko**mi
sad	wem	seat	**be**flo
sadden	we**me**ka	second	**be**vo
saddle	**sa**do	secret	twar
safe	**sa**fek	section	kipe**kev**
safety	safe**k**wi	secure	**sa**fuz
saga	**wa**be	security	safuzune
said	yin**e**ka	seduce	aji**klu**
sake	at**u**ot	seductress	aji**kli**za
salad	Ћre**bu**	see	wu
sale	**ku**le	seek	wut
salt	sat	seem	wum
salty	**sa**tu	seen	wu**e**ka
same	gopet**e**ku	select	**za**bo
sans	sans	selection	zaboekev
sarong	nuil**o**di	self	**mi**rum
sashay	**no**tik	sell	**ku**le
Saturday	Satu**s**dum	semester	si**san**da
save	**sa**yek	senate	hamlj
say	yin	senator	hamlj**oe**
scandal	**sku**Ћtu	send	uka**zo**
scare	**ro**ding	sensation	naji**nekev**
scarf	**flu**fa	sense	**na**jin

sensual	najin**odi**	shoot	**fra**ix
sensuous	na**ji**nu	shoot	**twe**ni
sentence	dueko	shop	**si**fla
sentiment	**dum**bex	short	**hun**jo
sentimental	dum**be**xid	shorts	**hun**jos
separate	huH**pis**le	should	**y**oni
September	**Ten**ka	shoulder	ebun
serenity	sere**nu**ne	shout	**kir**ni
series	hunap	show (n)	**das**da
serious	**sdif**lun	show (v)	**bu**ja
serve	renj	shower	HiH
service	**ren**ju	showoff	**bu**jau
session	duHekev	shred	abodo
set	**se**fer	shrub	**ked**wa
setting	sefer**ma**ki	shy	**ta**bey
settle	gole**mo**	sick	**wi**ge
seventh	sep**ou**	side	to
sever	huH**pis**le	sidekick	**to**kik
several	huHpisle**odi**	sigh	blin
sex	**xa**ji	sign	**gi**wi
sexy	xa**ji**u	silence	sile**wa**
shabby	**di**sar	silly	**kou**
shade	kuli**gas**	silver	vi**jir**
shake	**jo**te	simple	**ye**ra
shape	geH**ua**	simply	yera**u**
share	jin	since	**hu**ti
sharp	**ki**se	sing	pom
sharp	Hap	single	**ge**nik
she	**en**in	sink	**ne**ok
sheet	gaya**wi**	sirens	sdal
shelf	**hi**ta	sister	**ke**ki
shift	**fla**nu	sit	**be**tam
shine	ru	situation	betamu**ekev**
shirt	**ax**is	sixth	**si**su
shoe	fub	size	afodil

skill	ezuli	society	wedune
skin	eblin	sock (n)	oya
skinny	eblinu	sock (v)	fup
skip	gdami	soft	sese
skirt	plis	soldier	faroe
skit	plos	solid	lile
sky	sdaja	solidify	lilepeo
slap	ome	solution	ukonjekev
slave	jekine	solve	ukonj
slavery	jekineaHe	some	dok
sleep	yat	somehow	dokspleyn
sleeve	egide	someone	dokpik
slight	bimya	something	dokapgo
slim	bin	sometime	dokemi
slow	jakiHi	somewhere	dokerem
small	baznu	son	jevat
smart	dazu	song	pomu
smell	mibla	soon	aodo
smile	heki	sorry	vyu
smuggle	katife	sort	migu
smuggler	katifoe	soul	eyuri
snack	plin	sound	adi
snake	sdan	sour	lea
snappy	snapu	source	kirwik
sneak	katife	South	usij
sneer	snir	southern	usijaze
sniper	katfraix	souvenir	suvenin
snore	klog	space	flo
snow	sdo	Spain	Spayn
snowball	sdonix	span	sdas
so	vi	spare	biyeko
soak	amoj	spawn	sdaH
soap	adni	speak	nub
soccer	sokoe	special	zaneka
social	wedoj	speed	rey

spend	**ska**baz	steady	sdeneu
spill	spiln	steady	**tea**d
spin	**til**me	steal	**di**ko
spirit	**pe**ki	stealth	suliu
split	**ko**pep	steam	**bli**ag
sponsor	sdeH̶oe	stem	uhev
sport	fyi	stench	**fi**sa
spot	**te**ga	step	**di**ab
spotlight	tegimya	stereotypes	H̶renesyen
spread	zom	stick	**so**ta
spree	fameko	sticky	**so**tau
Spring	umle	still	**hi**ki
spring (v)	ku	stomach	**kyo**gis
sprinkle	**ku**ma	stop	**ne**mip
spiritualist	pe**ki**zi	store	**zir**va
spy	**vi**ki	story	diH̶e
square	**bla**ka	straight	**ro**pi
squeeze	siu	stranded	mlix
stable	**po**ni	strange	**do**mi
stage	**da**bun	stranger	domioe
stand	tan	strap	xetag
standard	key	strategy	ratalu
star	**smas**dun	stream	**sa**s**da**
store	smas	street	**ko**jem
stark	a**go**six	strength	**hu**mar
start	**mo**mla	stress	**im**fas
startle	mlat	stretch	**sduru**H̶
state	**bia**ta	stride	mey
statehood	bia**tes**os	strike	ome
statement	bat**a**bex	string	**hu**maz
statistic	H̶uli**aze**	stripe	**ban**ya
statue	**pye**tan	strive	**ye**tra
status	**ta**na	strong	hum
stay	**ne**mip	struggle	zidaH̶
steady	**sdene**	strut	**wed**ej

student	gdatavoe	surface	**sur**pey
studious	gda**ta**vu	surprise	surda**H**a
study	**gda**tav	surround	su**ro**nde
stuff	**su**fa	survey	wul**a**klj
stumble	**twa**ble	suspect	**pu**dom
style	**sdi**lo	suspicion	pudomekev
style	sma	suspicious	pud**o**mu
subject	**val**palit	swagger	xoe
submit	**vala**Ħ	swallow	**ig**dem
subsist	val**e**kev	sweat	es**oro**s
subtraction	baz**e**kev	sweater	es**oro**es
suburb	**val**ud	sweet	**i**bi
suburban	valu**d**an	swell	mi**fa**Ħa
succeed	box**a**go	swivel	wey
success	**bo**xum	symbol	**he**su
such	**a**do	sympathetic	hes**weu**
suck	tok	sympathy	**he**swe
sudden	**gda**bi	system	labu**h**ev
suddenly	gda**bi**u	**T**	
suffer	**tumf**te	table	fuam
suffrage	tumf**te**jag	tabloid	**nu**gun
suggest	Ħakod	take	moveĦi
suit	ku**fu**ga	talent	**brim**ta
summer	**zo**braj	talk	nub
summon	**kis**in	tan	gey
sun	**sdun**si	tangle	**ag**ag
Sunday	sisd**u**me	tank	**wa**ri
sunny	sdun**s**iu	task	ab**o**do
super	sder	tax	**tan**ge
supermarket	**sder**blir	taxi	**ta**xi
supervisor	sde**woe**	teach	fli**o**nde
supply	**fli**go	team	**la**ke
support	pod**a**ri	tear	**zi**Ħi
sure	sun	tedious	**go**go
surf	pey	teenage	wos**mi**du

telephone	nuis	therapeutic	twenjetaze
television	telewuekev	therapy	twenjetu
tell	nudu	there	sazuj
temporary	hunfaHe	therefore	sazujmar
tempt	huneka	these	His
temptation	hunevekev	they	tey
tend	hudnu	thick	bovi
tennis	tenez	thin	bin
tense	bapi	thing	apgo
tensile	babin	think	ratun
tent	gdalej	third	treu
tenth	dejeu	thirst	gdanka
term	xeka	thirsty	gdankau
terrible	rodible	this	tis
terrify	sderopeo	those	tos
terrorism	rodingzim	though	tenko
terrorist	rodingoe	thought (n)	gokevinum
test	flungo	threat	feban
text	jebix	thrill	badij
textile	jugda	throat	juga
texture	jenufte	through	blos
than	tan	throughout	blosnine
thank	gdasije	throw	wohi
that	tat	thud	dup
the	ta	thumb	idote
theater	plonzoe	thunder	tunder
theatric	plonzu	Thursday	Artsdum
theatrical	plonzuodi	ticket	trenu
theft	dogla	tides	mod
their	ih'tey	tie	kine
them	tem	tight	baga
themselves	temirum	time	emi
then	ten	timid	tabey
theory	teris	tiny	afanu
therapist	twenjetizi	tire	broy

tired	broyeka	travel	**le**var
to	ka	treasure	**ge**nin
today	kas**du**me	treat	**ve**Hask
toes	**to**naj	tree	brun
together	ma**kau**	trend	**pla**ma
tolerant	zou**mau**	trendy	plam**au**
tolerate	**zo**ulj	trial	**ze**dodi
tomorrow	ka**e**ko	triangle	**sla**kun
tonic	**bla**wi	tribute	**bra**jma
tonight	ka**be**slum	trillion	Hmild**e**di
too	rix	trouble	bad**e**mi
top	**dya**ki	truck	**ma**bri
toss	migda	true	**wa**fe
total	nik**a**ma	truly	waf**eu**
tough	**twu**vu	trust	**do**ni
tour	**o**sta	truth	waf**eu**
tourist	ostizi	try	zed
tow	**sno**mu	tub	**wu**be
toward	**ka**Ha	Tuesday	Mercusdum
town	**to**ne	tune	**po**nil
toy	fle	turn	sup**ine**
track	lak	twice	dita
trade	**blu**ti	twin	**di**tup
tradition	tradeke**vo**di	twist	wist
trail	**ha**le	type	syen
train	guv**e**hi	typical	**syen**odi
trainer	guvehi**o**e	**U**	
trample	**ve**hask	ultimate	**me**milj
transform	trof**go**bet	unable	**ne**ble
transformation	trofgobet**e**kev	uncomfortable	nesin**mo**ble
translate	**trof**yolf	uncover	**ne**gdiln
translation	trofyo**e**kev	undeniable	nedor**ne**bla
transparent	wublou	under	ne**do**e
trauma	av**e**ha	underground	ne**do**ding
traumatize	**ave**halj	understand	lo**ir**tan

underwear	nedokuvip	version	hesuekev
union	pislao	very	vi
unit	pisle	veteran	osmadoe
united	pisleka	victory	veato
universe	pibum	video	video
university	pibumune	vigor	hin
unlike	nelika	vigorous	hinu
unperturbed	neiribla	vigorously	hinu
until	rum	vile	bilHi
untrue	newafe	village	kijiji
unusual	nemlamir	villain	bilon
up	sip	violence	bilint
update	sipHemi	violent	bilont
upon	siplad	virtual	xuminid
upset	vurpue	virtually	xuminidu
urban	udan	virtue	xumine
urge	urj	visa	visa
us	jas	vision	wuekev
use	him	visit	swir
usual	mlamir	vital	lati
usually	mlamiru	voice	kyem
V		void	piem
vacant	amtont	volunteer	tuazum
vacate	amtlj	vote	twango
vacation	amtekev	voter	twangoe
vagina	aeganej	vow	dafu
value	tale	vulnerable	zoubla
vanilla	vanila	vulnerability	zoublaune
variety	hesune	**W**	
vary	hesu	waif	bina
veer	wanomi	wail	mlaoa
vegetable	bul	waist	hiln
vein	haH	wait	giwa
vendor	kuloe	waiter	giwoe
verse	bum	walk	giab

wall	**ga**bey	which	**i**mos
wallet	**wa**gum	while	ogi
wander	**ka**mul	whisk	**ku**rer
want	kamoe	whiskey	**wi**ski
war	gir	whisper	ga**to**hi
warm	**fle**jot	white	jux
warn	gir**ashi**	whittle	**ho**yi
was	sy**eka**	who	ken
wash	**fe**bin	whole	**fra**gda
watch	fod	why	**ga**la
water	o**atwa**	wide	**gu**lun
way	ved	wife	on**a**bu
we	jas	wife	**ta**ma
weak	**ama**	will (n)	min
weakness	amawi	win	**ne**nub
weapon	**so**jwa	wind	wuꞪ
wear	**ku**vip	wind (v)	wist
weather	klilj	window	kad**a**baz
wedding	ven**maki**	wings	ings
Wednesday	**Vens**dum	winner	nenuboe
week	**ja**ta	winter	**ver**na
weekend	jut**azo**	wise	**da**da
weight	**twa**pa	wish	ni**nin**
welcome	bir**ulin**	with	u**li**
well	bi	without	u**li**ne
went	mip**eka**	woman	u**ma**
were	sy**eka**	wonder	**a**fley
West	**mag**anij	won't	ne**umo**
wet	o**ato**	wood	prin
what	**ki**mey	word	eda
wheels	ef**edua**	work	**la**bo
when	**tie**m	world	**fa**ye
where	**erem**	worry	Ɜ**ro**ja
wherever	erem**eki**	worse	**badz**ba
whether	Ɜ**o**pi	worth	**ple**lin

worthy	plel**inu**	yet	goH̵
would	**um**on	you	pu
wound	**e**mar	young	**ro**kip
wrap	edidi	your	**ih**'pu
write	ite	youth	ro**ki**u
written	i**te**ka	yuppies	yups
wrong	**r**itra		

Y

zip   H̵ip

ya'll	pun**i**nom	zipper H̵i**poe**
year	am**e**mo	
yearn	**do**yej	
yellow	**ka**ro	
yes	ye	
yesterday	osmi**dume**	

Z

Ħodaoa-Anibo Order

A

a	a
abaz	breeze
abe	loose
ableyem	jingle
ableyem	institute
ableyemekev	institution
ablun	award
abodo	shred
abodo	task
adaoa	acclaim
adaun	amount
adi	sound
adni	soap
ado	such
adyabla	available
adyak	avail
aeganej	vagina
aer	aware
afa	blink
afanu	tiny
afley	wonder
afodil	size
afoti	credit
afula	catch
aga	even
agag	tangle

agatuodi	eventual
agenjag	advantage
agepa	agree
agoja	dozen
agosdi	anarchy
agosix	stark
aĦ	as
ahudekev	attention
ahudnu	attend
ais	genuine
ajami	pajamas
aje	fame
ajega	family
ajegir	familiar
ajeu	famous
ajeu	renown
ajikliza	seductress
ajiklu	seduce
ajit	bag
ajitu	baggy
ajote	fire
ajujul	principle
ajum	prince
ajumiza	princess
akafe	century
akat	cent
akinaga	ache
ako	lull
akog	apart
akogbex	apartment
akomi	lullaby

akrobat	acrobat
akwetlu	glide
aler	few
aliar	account
alkinawi	business
alko	busy
aludlj	arrest
alupun	accord
alupunmaki	according
ama	weak
amajukint	mathematic
amatwa	pain
amawi	weakness
amej	bliss
amemlj	apologize
amemo	year
amemodi	annual
amemu	apology
Ameriki	American
amoj	soak
amorint	romance
amoshex	amusement
amotu	match
amtekev	vacation
amtip	empty
amtlj	vacate
amtont	vacant
an	at
anba	best
anda	month
andye	lock

ane	better
anebex	improvement
Aneka	April
anso	adore
ansoekev	adoration
anvuHato	persuade
anwega	precise
anwekev	precision
aodo	soon
apgo	thing
apiem	avoid
apikya	isolated
apue	role
ari	opinion
arik	opera
Art	Earth
artir	cling
Artsdum	Thursday
asey	drift
asilin	approach
askanij	north
asli	run
asuazim	across
aswakau	develop
ata	bruise
atili	churn
ativlu	petal
ato	mix
atoe	border
atuot	benefit
atuot	sake

atuotlj	beneficial	azyekevu	creativity
auban	effort		

B

audix	method	babin	tensile
audixaze	methodic	babri	fix
audixazeu	methodically	babrilj	fixate
aved	away	babriljekev	fixation
avedo	motivate	bademi	trouble
avedoekev	motivation	badij	thrill
aveha	trama	badz	bad
avehalj	traumatize	badzba	worse
awega	appoint	bafeni	penis
awegabex	appointment	baga	tight
axe	break	baH	bash
axiet	anxious	bahuekev	identification
axietu	anxiety	bahuklu	identify
axis	axis	baibin	plate
axis	shirt	baig	fly
axni	intrude	baigava	flight
axnioe	intruder	bajun	dance
ayn	merge	bal	fine
Aza	God	baledo	ecstatic
Azejimi	Christmas	banaya	banana
azen	accent	bani	mean
azgaoe	character	banil	line
azifte	literature	banya	stripe
azni	lesson	bapi	tense
aznu	hold	bari	of
azye	create	barum	broom
azyej	child	batabex	statement
azyejiz	children	bati	father
azyejsos	childhood		

ba**vy**ika	grotesque	**bi**lont	violent
ba**ze**kev	subtraction	bi**mai**	recline
bazne	less	**bim**ya	slight
baznu	small	bin	slim
beflo	seat	bin	thin
bega	letter	**bi**na	waif
be**li**fid	immortal	**bi**not	chest
be**li**fidlj	immortalize	bi**pa**ri	chair
be**lo**le	fat	**bi**po	bottom
bem	half	bir	beer
bembri	arch	bi**ru**lin	welcome
bem**le**pli	haphazard	bis	raise
ben	mine (n)	bix	gun
beok	carry	bi**ye**ko	spare
beosa**pug**da	executive	biyo**ket**ont	prominent
bera	buy	bla	able
bersi	inquire	**bla**boz	obstacles
beslum	night	**blak**a	square
betam	sit	**bla**min	divide
beta**mue**kev	situation	**bla**wi	tonic
bevo	second	**blen**up	final
bi	well	**blen**up	finale
bi**a**ta	state	**bleu**ne	ability
bia**tes**os	statehood	**bli**ag	steam
bidar	grow	blin	sigh
biꟼoket	decide	blir	market
biꟼo**ket**ev	decision	blit	air
bilꟼi	vile	blit	bleat
bilint	violence	blon**odi**	colonial
bilmla	assault	blos	blouse
bilon	villain	blos	through

blosnine	throughout
blulir	danger
bluliru	dangerous
blum	adopt
blum	bloom
blun	breath
bluti	exchange
bluti	trade
bod	bother
boron	brown
bovi	thick
bovu	callous
boxago	succeed
boxum	success
braba	bead
brajma	tribute
brak	caution
brak	care
brakaHe	cautionary
braku	cautious
brata	honor
bri	ring
brimta	talent
brint	preach
brisa	rise
broy	tire
broyeka	tired
brun	tree
buf	buff
buja	show (v)
bujau	showoff

bujekev	illustration
bujetlj	illustrate
bujinu	illuminous
bujirlj	illuminate
buk	board
bul	vegetable
bula	behind
bulamot	after
bulamotvo	afterward
bulanopau	afternoon
bulat	early
bulin	back
bulinsem	backpack
bulo	attire
bulo	dress
bum	verse
bunoe	hinder
bunup	odd

D

dabdar	bra
dabej	breast
dabun	stage
dada	wise
dafu	echo
dafu	vow
dajir	offer
daka	mild
dal	promise
danHa	prize
danil	autumn

danil	fall (n)	diato	parade
daoa	claim	dibajag	offense
dari	port	dibazo	offend
dasda	portray	dibazpugda	offensive
dasda	show (n)	dibela	awkward
dat	dot	dibey	off
date	lib	didni	fax
datelj	liberate	diet	diet
dateodi	liberal	difit	bicep
dazeko	intellect	difu	drop
dazekolj	intellectual	digowe	reveal
dazekond	intelligent	diHe	story
dazu	smart	diko	steal
debu	debated	dind	real
defe	attract	dindipau	reality
defoe	hammer	dindlj	realize
dej	bless	dindu	really
dejede	decade	ding	ground
dejeu	tenth	dint	patience
dek	drum	dionde	bicycle
delinj	peek	dip	dip
demokramla	democracy	dip	dive
demokraze	democratic	dipo	piece
demuk	medal	disar	shabby
dera	gender	dismilit	paranoia
deraze	genetic	dismilitoe	paranoid
derekev	generation	dita	twice
derney	gene	ditana	couple
dernlj	moderate	ditana	pair
dernu	modern	dite	drip
diab	step	ditu	duo

ditup	twin	dor**ma**rek	decrease
diya	fund	**do**rne	deny
diya	money	doro**klj**	demise
do**ak**a	percent	**do**rum	deflect
dofa**H**ont	giant	**do**rwan	descent
dogla	theft	dor**yo**fe	delude
doin	mark	dor**yofey**kev	delusion
dok	some	**do**yej	yearn
dok**ap**go	something	du**e**ko	sentence
dok**ek**ev	portion	du**H**ekev	session
dok**e**mi	sometime	dul	blood
dok**e**rem	somewhere	du**le**ka	bleed
doklo	rain	dulgdan**kau**	bloodthirsty
doklo-**bem**bri	rainbow	dum	feel
dokpik	someone	**dum**bex	sentiment
dokspleyn	somehow	dum**bex**id	sentimental
domax	quest	duna**H**e	ordinary
do**max**ev	question	dundi**e**kev	collection
domi	strange	**du**nu	order
dom**i**oe	stranger	dup	thud
do**na**da	fold	**du**pun	get
do**na**ze	blemish	dupun**e**ka	got
doni	trust	**dya**ki	top
dorbal	define	**dya**ku	ambitious
dorbal**ek**ev	definition	**dy**en	miss
dore**jag**	detail	**dyu**ne	quality
dore**poa**	detain	dyu**peo**	qualified
dorla**H**i	deject	**E**	
dorla**H**i	depress	e**alu**	degree
dorla**H**i**ekev**	depression	e**az**	duty
dorlak	detract		

ebarba	least
eblin	skin
eblinu	skinny
ebri	pray
ebrioe	prayer
ebu	again
ebuba	against
ebun	shoulder
eda	word
edamik	loud
edamoku	loudly
edidi	wrap
edikoizi	plagiarist
edikozim	plagiarism
efedua	wheels
efele	disturb
egide	sleeve
egim	hurt
ejenamla	fantasy
ejenata	fanatic
ejenti	phantom
ejeplik	fancy
ejimi	gift
ejma	give
ejpo	rare
ekagix	email
ekenizuj	beyond
ekev	be
ekev	exist
ekeveka	been
ekevgda	behavior

eki	ever
ekiu	every
ekiupik	everyone
ekiwa	juice
eko	future
ekond	evolve
ekot	address
eli	fill
eli	full
elili	fulfill
elsip	hire
emar	wound
emer	Airplanes
emi	time
enata	risk
enejedip	energy
enejedlj	energize
enejedu	energetic
eney	he
enimuse	inspire
enimusekev	inspiration
enin	she
enmotega	enforce
enmotegabex	enforcement
eoa	bile
epli	pepper
eran	paper
erem	where
eremeki	wherever
esay	escape
eskomla	school

esor**oes** — sweater
esor**os** — sweat
est — eager
estwi — eagerness
eta**k**i — cousin
ev**H**evun — befriend
ev**o**ri — groove
evpedonj — because
ev**rel**in — become
evto — aside
evto — beside
evu**H** — between
ewe**g**a — point
ey — hey
eyaf — prestige
eyafu — prestigious
eyera — honey
eyeuri — soul
e**zin**se — butt
e**zu**li — skill
e**zu**toe — handicap

F

fa — or
fabaz — many
fablu — gusto
fa**H**abaz — big
fa**H**abaz — large
faliar — abroad
fa**l**ine — far
fali**noe** — further
fama — much

fameko — spree
fanin — old
fa**os**mej — orphan
faosmiejag — orphanage
farem — button
faroe — soldier
fas**dif**te — manufacture
faye — world
feban — threat
febin — wash
fed**o**di — federal
fe**dua** — heel
femu — fumble
fen — minor
fent — grain
fentu — grainy
fen**uma** — female
fenu**maze** — feminine
fenu**mizi** — feminist
fenu**mzim** — feminism
fen**u**ne — minority
feralj — penetrate
fer**H** — heal
ferHu — health
fey — minute
fiaj — jail
fisa — stench
flaf — fluff
flafu — fluffy
flanu — shift
flaya — hope

flay**a**el	hopeful
fle	toy
flejot	warm
fligo	supply
flini	enough
fli**on**de	instruct
fli**on**de	teach
fli**onde**dev	instruction
flir	inch
flit	flutter
flo	space
flo**numa**ki	during
fluey	firm
flufa	scarf
flum	mass
flum**pug**da	massive
flungo	test
fod	watch
fodix	mission
fodor	focus
fosa	pose
fosakefte	posture
fose**kev**	position
fos**ki**lan	scout
fos**ye**a	positive
fos**y**ible	possible
fra**g**da	whole
fraix	shoot
Frans	France
FrenH	French
fua	drink

fuam	booth
fuam	table
fub	shoe
fuba	fight
fula	cookie
fup	sock (v)
fuz	fuzz
fya	main
fya**sas**da	mainstream
fye**poa**	maintain
fye**si**raze	automatic
fye**su**ya	automobile
fyi	sport

G

gabey	wall
gablu	artificial
gablu	fake
gablu	faux
gabos	fraud
gabuba	enemy
gada	fast
gada	mud
gada	quick
gadine	fashion
gagun	page
gaHote	ride
gaj	dodge
gakau	perfect
gakauekev	perfection
gakay	nail

ga**ki**zi	persist	**gda**ye	junk
ga**ku**baz	crowd	**gde**da	grab
gaku**kau**	folklore	**gdef**da	about
gaku**ka**zo	present	**gde**fe	bring
gakup	person	**gde**ga	bed
gaku**po**di	personal	gdega **ku**lat	bedroom
gakupo**diu**	personally	gden	passion
gakupo**dune**	personality	gdi**ek**ev	fiction
ga**ku**twa	perhaps	**gdi**ka	rug
gala	why	gdiln	cover
gam	feed	gdim	preside
ganom	corner	gdi**mo**e	president
gapit	deal	gdimoemla	presidency
gari	game	**gdo**hint	battle
gar**li**ne	next	**gdo**me	help
gatohi	whisper	gdu	floor
gavi	key	gdub	awake
gawars	flowers	**gdu**hi	play
gayawi	sheet	gduhioe	player
gazu	here	gdu**hi**te	playwright
gdabi	sudden	**gdu**nuj	kitchen
gda**bi**u	suddenly	gef	bet
gdalej	tent	geℍ**ua**	shape
gdami	skip	**ge**le	proud
gdanka	thirst	**ge**len	pride
gdan**kau**	thirsty	gen	own
gdar	dream	**ge**nik	single
gda**si**je	thank	genin	treasure
gdatav	study	**ge**nu	only
gda**tav**oe	student	gey	tan
gda**ta**vu	studious	**gi**ab	walk

gila	elect
gilae**kev**	election
gin	gin
gina	critic
ginaodi	critical
gingoe	ginger
gini	favor
gini**ba**	favorite
gir	war
gira**shi**	warn
gitar	guitar
giwa	wait
giwi	sign
gi**woe**	waiter
giye	good
gobet	form
gobe**todi**	formal
gobe**toe**	former
godo	move
go**do**bex	movement
gogo	tedious
gogob**c**ta	format
goꞪ	yet
goke	believe
goket	belief
goke**vin**um	thought (n)
go**ko**ble	credible
go**ko**vo	credit
go**ko**vont	credential
go**ko**vwi	credibility
golemo	settle

go**pet**eku	same
go**pet**um	repeat
goro	lunch
go**ru**pem	crew
gos	ghost
gota	often
goveꞪiumo	retrieve
govu	govern
govubex	government
govuoe	governor
gowu	revise
gowue**kev**	revision
goye**lun**	movie
guak	dare
guay	grey
gubir	broad
guesu	bride
gulun	wide
gumla	gentle
guvehi	train
guvehioe	trainer

h

ha	dub
habo	screen
hadiꞪe	history
hadi**tiekev**	fabrication
hadi**til**j	fabricate
hafla	bid
haꞪ	vein
haka	crazy

hale	path	
hale	trail	
hami	both	
hamlj	senate	
hamlj**oe**	senator	
hanҴuni	handsome	
han**i**ba	July	
hanlo	rattle	
hap	drop	
hap**i**mey	paint	
ha**po**jen	painting (n)	
hara	lot	
hari	basket	
harinix	basketball	
hask	harsh	
hasova**j**ekev	hallucination	
ha**so**vajlj	hallucinate	
hatav	horse	
hatҴe	February	
havi	hang	
havlu	ethnic	
havlune	ethnicity	
haz	arm	
heki	smile	
hent	hint	
heraҴ	profess	
heraҴoe	professor	
her**ave**	promote	
hera**zizi**	protagonist	
herdon	problem	
herҴi	project	

herip	program
herki	product
herklu	produce
hermin	provide
herno	probe
herno**ble**	probable
herno**blu**	probably
her**petek**	profound
herpo	frenzy
herspiekev	protection
hersyenodi	prototypical
heruҴa	progress
heruҴa**ekev**	progressive
hesu	logo
hesu	symbol
hesu	vary
he**sue**kev	version
he**su**ne	variety
heswe	sympathy
hes**weu**	sympathetic
heto	rust
hey	polish
higu	film
hiҴni	chuckle
hijes	lip
hiki	still
hiln	waist
him	use
himon	lift
hin	vigor
hini	guess

hinu	vigorous
hinu	vigorously
hinuba	estimate
hinubekev	estimation
hispani	hispanic
hita	shelf
hitem	hide
hitib	code
honaj	finger
honris	accept
hovi	heat
hoyi	carve
hoyi	whittle
hublodi	potential
hubri	hard
hudnu	tend
huHagepa	disagree
huHagepa	dissent
huHagepaoe	dissenter
huHagepaoe	dissident
huHaweg	disappointment
huHfablu	disgust
huHlak	distract
huHpi	décor
huHpilj	decorate
huHpisle	separate
huHpisle	sever
huHpisleodi	several
huHsdepebla	discourage
huHsinit	disappear
huHtufa	disgrace

huHyem	displace
huHyokem	denounce
huluj	challenge
hum	strong
humar	strength
humaz	string
hunap	series
huneHemo	harassed
huneka	tempt
hunevekev	temptation
hunfaHe	temporary
hunjo	short
hunjos	shorts
huti	since

Ĥ

Ĥakod	suggest
Ĥano	channel
Ĥap	sharp
Ĥapodit	damage
Ĥaron	now
Ĥas	pursuit
Ĥat	chat
Ĥatoe	chatter
Ĥaye	moment
Ĥemi	date
Ĥenix	do
Ĥeniye	done
Ĥeniye	finish
Ĥeok	horror
Ĥeokble	horrible

Ħ**es**	hiss	Ħo**ej**ma	reward
Ħ**ev**uns	friends	Ħo**ej**ma**ki**	rewarding
Ħ**ev**unwi	friendship	Ħo**ek**ond	revolve
Ħ**ewi**gag	hospital	Ħo**ek**on**ek**ev	revolution
Ħ**i**	clean	Ħo**ek**on**ek**evu	revolutionary
Ħ**ie**go	clear	Ħo**e**po**a**	retain
Ħ**ie**goba	clearest	Ħ**o**fai	prison
Ħ**ie**gune	clarity	Ħ**o**fi	receive
ĦiĦ	shower	Ħ**o**fi**pugda**	receptive
ĦiĦ **ku**lat	bathroom	Ħo**gakukazo**	represent
Ħ**i**j	dark	Ħo**gakukazo**e	representative
Ħ**i**p	zip	Ħ**o**gdiln	recover
Ħ**i**poe	zipper	Ħ**o**gek	respect
Ħ**i**r'	pick	Ħo**gi**wi	resign
Ħ**i**s	these	Ħo**gi**win**ek**ev	resignation
Ħmild**e**di	trillion	Ħo**gn**ama	nickname
Ħ**mil**nop	billion	Ħo**go**bet	reform
Ħ**o**ad	reason	Ħo**go**do	remove
Ħ**o**aĦ	remit	Ħo**go**po**diu**	habitually
Ħo**brad**it	refer	Ħo**go**pu	habit
Ħo**bre**it	recent	Ħo**go****pu**an	habitat
Ħo**d**ar	report	ĦoĦi	reject
Ħo**d**ar**oe**	reporter	ĦoĦiekev	rejection
Ħo**de**is	response	Ħo**jo**nu	research
Ħo**do**in	remark	Ħok	choke
Ħo**do**in**a**bla	remarkable	Ħo**ka**te	remember
Ħo**do**ka**pugda**	relative	Ħo**kis**pir	regard
Ħo**do**kat	relate	Ħo**k**lu	reduce
Ħo**do**kevwi	relationship	Ħo**la**Ħi	repress
ĦoduĦ	recess	Ħ**o**lak	retract
Ħoefe	rescue	Ħ**o**me	home

Ḥomlaf	regain	Ḥrep	cut
Ḥomri	restore	Ḥroja	worry
Ḥona	relax	Ḥua	joy
ḤoneḤen	refuse	Ḥuba	number
Ḥonin	remind	Ḥugomey	flow
Ḥopal	require	Ḥugomey	pump
Ḥopi	whether	ḤuḤ	hush
Ḥopluaze	republic	Ḥuliaze	statstic
Ḥora	repute		
Ḥoraka	react	**I**	
Ḥorakekev	reaction	ibi	sweet
Ḥorekev	reputation	idote	thumb
Ḥorum	reflect	iey	rich
Ḥorumekev	reflection	igdem	swallow
Ḥosdeble	responsible	ih'eney	his
Ḥosdeli	respond	ih'enin	her
Ḥosin	resent	ih'jas	our
Ḥosinel	resentful	ih'pas	mine
Ḥosupine	return	ih'pu	your
Ḥotal	retail	imfas	stress
Ḥoto	reside	imlakari	exploit
Ḥotoe	resident	imon	excuse
Ḥotoebex	residence	imos	which
Ḥotrima	religion	imperiodizim	imperialism
Ḥoune	recall	impir	expire
Ḥoyeha	reaffirm	impirekev	expiration
Ḥoyem	replace	implaka	explicit
Ḥoyokip	renew	implaki	explore
Ḥozir	record	implakiekev	exploration
Ḥrebu	salad	implawabip	explode
Ḥrenesyen	stereotypes	imri	adjust

imya	light
in**gine**	another
Ingle**H**	English
ings	wings
int	each
iras	matter
ira**so**di	material
i**ri**bla	perturb
iron	iron
Ita**li**n	Italian
Ita**lu**	Italy
ite	write
itef	graph
itefa**niti**	graffiti
ite**H**anu	notary
it**ek**a	written
it**e**nu	message
it**e**nu	note
it**e**nu	notice
iteslu	print
ix	if

J

jab	fan
jagda	bitter
ja**ji**kis	panties
jajis	pants (n)
ja**jo**e	brief
jajoetot	briefcase
jaki**H**i	slow
jakonj	balcony
jani	frown

jas	us
jas	we
jata	week
jazad	grant
jebix	text
jeki	daughter
je**ko**ne	slave
jekonea**H**e	slavery
jele	book
jem	gymnasium
jenu	hand
je**nu**el	handful
je**nuf**te	texture
jete	elbow
jevat	son
jey	immune
jufa	jaunt
jey**ye**le	music
jin	jean
jin	share
jirond	opportunity
jonu	search
jote	shake
jotz	hot
juga	throat
jugda	textile
junal	journal
jun**te**ba	journalist
Ju**pis**dum	Friday
ju**ta**vu	journey
juta**zo**	weekend

jux — white

K

ka — to
kabeslum — tonight
kabla — adapt
kadabaz — window
kadefi — quadriceps
kadu — fourth
kaeko — tomorrow
kaet — interest
kafe — café
kagix — mail
kaHa — toward
kalsesi — peach
kamoe — want
kamo — aspire
kamma — lust
kanimla — church
kanimla kenin — pastor
kap — ikon
kapuekev — function
kapuHino — cappuccino
karo — yellow
karoron — alive
kartavi — blonde
kasdume — today
kate — memory
katfraix — sniper
katife — smuggle
katife — sneak
katifoe — smuggler

katije — memoir
katirgu — category
katun — cartoon
kavehi — car
kavehi kulat — garage
kawedlj — associate
kayat — asleep
kaz — crash
kedwa — shrub
keH — cheek
keki — sister
ken — who
kenbu — attitude
kenflej — hat
kenin — head
kera — clerk
kera — origin
kerkaodi — original
kerkoze — indigenous
key — awe
key — standard
ki — huge
kide — addict
kidekev — addiction
kiduH — obsess
kijiji — village
kijin — clue
kimey — what
kine — tie
kipekev — chunk
kipekev — section

kipo	brother
kirwik	source
kisaH	confess
kis**braj**ma	contribute
kisbrajma**ekev**	contribution
kise	sharp
kis**e**tot	conflict
kis**e**yu	consist
kisfit	concept
kis**fluey**	confirm
kisfluj	conclude
kis**flun**go	contest
kis**H**ibi	conspire
kis**H**ibioe	conspirator
kis**H**omi	convert
kisin	convene
kisin**ekev**	convention
kis**je**bix	context
kis**ka**et	concern
kisna**ji**nu	consensus
kis**n**int	confidence
kisnix	confide
kis**no**e	confer
kis**nont**	confidante
kispir	guard
kis**pi**twu	conscious
kis**ratlj	consider
kisren**pug**da	conservative
kisvelj	immediate
kisvelj	immediately
klap	clap
klasafu	guarantee
klato	class
Kleopa	August
kli	law
klioe	lawyer
klilj	climate
klo	cloud
klog	snore
klu	make
klu**pluaz**	publish
kobalt	cobalt
koe**odi**	particle
kog	part
ko**gaH**e	party
koga**nis**	parent
koge**kili**	particular
kojem	street
koj**mede**	food
kola**ga**	colleague
kolak	abstract
kola**klj**	advertise
kolej	college
kombe	cup
konka	plain
kongres	congress
kopep	split
ko**piem**	accident
koron **ku**lat	dinning room
koro**nis**	restaurants
kort	court
kou	silly

koukonan	absolute	labokazo	diploma
krak	crack	labokekev	diplomacy
ku	leap	labuhev	system
kua	rule	ladia	doorstep
kua	policy	ladit	on
kuazim	politic	laHiseta	press
kuazimodi	political	laHisetalj	pressure
kufte	culture	laj	law
kufuga	suit	lajodi	legal
kuja	grand	lak	track
kujabati	grandfather	lakat	rectangle
kujayeye	grandmother	lake	team
kul	cool	lakoz	career
kulat	room	lalo	area
kule	sell	laloke	achieve
kule	sale	lame	lick
kuligas	shade	lamejul	destiny
kuloe	vendor	lami	animal
kuma	sprinkle	lamirj	mirror
kundi	collect	lamoluj	parallel
kundi	gather	lamoz	almond
kunint	finance	lanuj	blame
kurer	whisk	lapa	land
kuvip	wear	lari	lawn
kwanuri	protest	lati	vital
kyem	voice	lavat	hunger
kyogis	stomach	lavatu	hungry
		lavmar	greed
		lavmaru	greedy
		lawa	amaze
		lawa	astonish

L

labin	exercise
labo	labor
labo	work

lea	sour	lo**i**ma	general
ledwa	lack	**lo**ir	over
ledwa**ma**ki	devoid	loir**ku**vip	accessories
le**fi**bo	masterpiece	loir**tan**	understand
lefij	great	loir**trevo**	overwhelm
legor	allege	loj	edit
legorekev	allegation	lo**jo**di	editorial
leji	ocean	lo**jo**e	editor
lemuk	hip	lol	roll
lepli	hazard	**lo**lir	routine
lesin	demand	**lon**kas	clothes
leti	link	lo**ro**i	curve
levar	travel	**lu**du	rest
levij	navel	luk	blue
ley	hip	lum	read
li	and	**lu**ne	moon
li**a**mu	deep	**Lun**sdum	Monday
liar	road	**lu**pun	cord
lika	like	lur	lure
lika**da**da	likewise	**lu**tum	heave
lile	solid	lu**tu**mu	heavy
lile**pe**o	solidify	**M**	
linj	dry	ma	any
lisa**oe**	banker	**ma**bri	truck
lisar	bank	**ma**fle	flame
lo	cloth	**mag**anij	West
lo**a**da	pleat	**ma**gaz	magazine
loga	distinct	**ma**gun	occupy
lo**gaze**	distinctive	maĦ	milk
logint	distance	maĦarij	east
logont	distant		

maĦjote	milkshake
maĦu	admit
maje	man
majeg	manage
majeyeoe	manpower
majix	curse
majmad	assure
makau	together
Makeda	June
makine	machine
mako	measure
maloji	breakfast
manlu	a.m.
manlu	morning
manoe	blister
maoaze	enthusiastic
maoe	all
maoved	always
maozim	enthusiasm
mapgo	anything
maplk	anyone
mar	add
mara	else
mara	more
marba	most
marekev	addition
marĦ	march
marines	marines
marinoe	council
marinub	consult
marinubont	consultant
martr	martyr
maryin	advice
maryin	advise
masinbaz	accompany
matron	matron
maumarba	almost
mave	loath
mawey	already
mazaz	climb
medoj	declare
meĦomi	change
meĦun	chance
meĦun	luck
meka	beauty
mekael	beautiful
memika	rave
memilj	maximum
memilj	ultimate
Mercusdum	Tuesday
mere	merit
mermi	liver
metabozim	metabolism
mey	stride
mibla	smell
mid	middle
midodi	central
midoe	center
mifaHa	swell
migda	toss
migu	sort
mikefin	perceive

mikefin**ekev**	perception
mi**la**dit	continue
mile	mile
mi**li**ne	leave
mima	clasp
mim**ar**po	abdomen
min	will (n)
minom	meet
mip	go
mip**e**ka	gone
mip**e**ka	went
mirko	luxury
mirum	self
misa	ear
mlaba	easy
mlada	beg
mlaf	gain
mlagan	corrupt
mlagan	immoral
mlak	abort
mlakekev	abortion
mlamir	usual
mla**mi**ru	usually
mlan	blend
mla**oa**	wail
mlar	beach
mlat	brass
mlat	startle
mle	little
mlebo	client
mlebo	clientele

mleH̱uni	cute
mleke	comb
mlenj	course
mlerH	perk
mleub	beat
mliajag	language
mlif	draw
mli**fa**va	gravity
mliflj	gravitate
mlix	stranded
mlo	build
mloH̱	building
mlokazu	incorporate
mlu	embrace
mlu	hug
mlur	blur
mod	tides
mofla	forbid
mogda	burn
mogdul	burgundy
mo**ken**in	forehead
moma	borrow
momla	start
mot	for
mo**tale**	fortune
mot**ba**bas	forefathers
mo**te**ga	force
mo**tej**ma	forgive
mo**te**ki	forever
motip	forge
mot**ma**bas	ancestors

motuĦa	advance
motuĦa	forward
motupun	forget
moveĦi	take
mukif	gasped
munje	green
munzawa	charisma
munzaze	charismatic
Musa	October
muyaye	could

N

nabsu	husband
nag	fish
nai	lay
najin	sense
najinekev	sensation
najinodi	sensual
najinu	sensuous
nalet	ballot
nama	name
namazne	anonymous
Nandi	December
naole	dog
nativ	native
ne	no
neapgo	nothing
neble	unable
nedoding	underground
nedoe	under
nedokuvip	underwear
nedornebla	undeniable

nefa	nor
Nefer	May (month)
nefu	confuse
negdiln	uncover
neHenabla	impossible
neĦi	never
neĦos	ignore
neĦosoe	ignorant
nehuĦplabla	inseparable
neiribla	unpreturb
nekogaze	nonpartisan
nelika	dislike
nelika	unlike
nemi	chronicle
nemip	stay
nemip	stop
nemlamir	unusual
nenub	win
nenuboe	winner
neok	sink
neokaz	abyss
neokaz	endless
neota	embarrass
nepik	no one
nepik	nobody
nepu	guest
neriĦ	neither
nerum	inflect
nesinmoble	uncomfortable
nesomnea	insomnia
nesyea	negative

neumo	won't	nikama	total
newafe	untrue	niklu	induce
neyokma	naïve	nikomi	season
neziaze	rhetoric	nimarek	increase
neziazu	rhetorically	nin	mind
ni	in	nine	out
nibamoe	encounter	ninekev	intention
nibapi	intense	nineto	outside
niblamiodi	individual	ninin	intend
nibo	poem	ninin	intent
niboe	poet	ninin	wish
nibovik	poetry	nipeki	instinct
nidari	import	nipinifu	injustice
nidariont	important	niponilj	intimate
nidiabekev	inauguration	nirelin	income
niekond	involve	nirev	invade
niferabla	impenetrable	nisagont	inherent
nifine	invoke	nisagvo	inherit
nifluj	include	nisagvojag	heritage
nigobet	inform	nisdene	instead
nigobetekev	information	niseyeka	inflamed
nigokabla	incredible	nisiti	inner-city
nihava	invite	nisoHis	innocent
niHogopuan	inhabitant	nitabelj	intimidate
niHua	enjoy	nito	inside
nija	image	nitoe	enter
nijapeo	imagine	nitoeHok	intercept
nijapeoekev	imagination	nitoeklu	introduce
nijefa	inmate	nitoenodi	internal
nik	chic	nitoeyolejodi	interracial
nika	into	nitoeyunanodi	international

nitojin	integrate		
nitopa	entertain	**O**	
nitoyunodi	international	oafte	moisture
nitrani	infuse	oag	river
nitubamoe	encounter	oajde	knee
nitwabla	inevitable	oapa	lake
niupiekev	independent	oato	moist
nix	ball	oato	wet
niyum	indeed	oatwa	water
nizaekev	immigration	oayn	emerge
nizaizi	immigrant	oaynimla	emergency
nizi	insist	obya	object
nizuj	foreign	octa	clip
nizujoe	foreigner	oduar	country
nopau	ninth	oer	pillow
nopau	noon	ogi	while
nopote	desire	oim	fit
notik	sashay	ojenis	art
nuafue	schedule	ojenisizi	artist
nub	speak	ojeta	article
nub	talk	ojuma	girl
nudu	tell	okar	edge
nue	leg	okau	eighth
nugun	tabloid	okazing	last
nuidorlj	elaborate	okazo	death
nuilodi	sarong	okazo	end
nuir	long	okH	cold
nuis	telephone	okHun	chill
nun	guide	okor	evil
nyeji	local	omaj	boy
nyelj	locate	omajHevun	boyfriend

ome	slap
ome	strike
omuir	anticipate
omuir	expect
onabu	wife
onde	circle
onde	cycle
onde	round
ondelj	circulate
ongyar	drama
ongyaru	dramatic
onz	ounce
ore	hour
osmad	experience
osmadoe	veteran
osmidueka	past (time)
osmidum	pass
osmidum	passport
osmidume	ago
osmidume	yesterday
osmipugda	passive
osta	tour
ostizi	tourist
osyokum	approve
ote	hit
owars	oar
oya	sock (n)
ozaHe	primary
ozuja	first
ozuja	prime

P

pa	me
pabo	face
paga	laugh
pagakon	clown
pahagdin	pace
paHedo	near
pal	ask
palat	nod
pali	scene
palijul	ideal
palit	idea
pamajag	footage
paman	foot
pamans	feet
pamirum	myself
patavye	brush
patri	brand
patrin	branch
patrinlj	franchize
patriotzim	patriotism
pauli	mystery
paz	calm
pea	pea
pedigri	pedigree
pedokaekev	education
pedokalj	educate
pedokaljeka	educated
pedonj	cause
peki	spirit
pekizi	spiritualist
pepo	keep

pepoa	obtain	plamla	comedy
petu	find	plamlai	comedian
petueka	found	plap	lodge
petuekaekev	foundation	plaset	flag
pey	surf	plaveji	bear
piad	item	plaze	comic
pibum	universe	pleit	copy
pibumune	university	plelin	appreciation
piem	void	plelin	worth
piHki	once	plelinu	worthy
piHu	loss	pleme	fall (v)
pimaje	human	pleta	follow
pimajepik	humanity	pletamaki	following
pimble	humble	plin	snack
pimey	color	plinit	itch
pini	just	plis	skirt
pinifu	justice	plismla	miniskirt
pinkum	arrive	ploha	glare
pislao	union	ploka	braid
pisle	unit	plong	marry
pisleka	united	plongjag	marriage
pisu	lose	plonzoe	theater
pisueka	lost	plonzu	theatric
plad	plaid	plonzuodi	theatrical
plaH	fun	plos	skit
plaHlj	joke	pluatune	publicity
plaHu	humor	pluaze	public
plakiewega	checkpoint	poak	park
plakli	check	poakmaki	parking
plama	trend	podama	askew
plamau	trendy	podari	support

podi	mess
podint	drug
pogda	might
pogda**u**	mighty
poji	meal
pol	poll
pole**ga**mu	polygamist
pole**ga**mu	polygamy
poli**so**e	police
pom	sing
pomu	song
poni	stable
ponil	tune
povo**da**	powder
pri**ma**son	permission
prin	wood
proHi	deputy
pu	you
pubaH	applesauce
pudom	suspect
pudom**ekev**	suspicion
pudo**mu**	suspicious
pugun	canvas
pum	apple
pu**ni**nom	ya'll
pya	rock
pya**ka**	rocket
pyetan	statue

R

ra	can
rablem	kidnap

ra**bu**deg	hell
rade	push
ra**dio**	radio
raf	ice
raka	act
ra**kag**	actual
ra**ka**gu	actually
rakapud**au**	activity
rakapugda**izi**	activist
rakapune	active
ra**ke**kev	action
ra**ko**e	actor
ra**ko**i	actress
ra**lo**san	legend
ram	occur
rama**bla**	miserable
rama**ga**	misery
ramint	occurrence
ramni	map
rane	cannot
ratalu	strategy
ratun	think
rau**oe**	minister
re**fi**les	rifle
re**fu**it	grapefruit
re**ko**nat	recognition
re**la**o	crawl
rele	compare
relin	come
relinot	attack
relun	compass

relunekev	compassion
renj	serve
renju	service
reti	pretty
rey	speed
ribix	conundrum
ribix	riddle
riꞪ	either
rint	reach
ritra	wrong
rix	also
rix	too
rixahu	rediculous
roaba	example
rod	rod
rodible	terrible
roding	freak
roding	scare
rodingoe	terrorist
rodingzim	terrorism
rodoe	monsters
rokibega	newsletter
rokiꞪe	novel
rokiꞪizi	novelist
rokip	new
rokip	young
rokiu	youth
roko	live (v)
roko kulat	livingroom
rokoze	life
rokozesma	lifestyle
rokozuja	begin
ronj	orange (color)
ronur	endure
ropi	straight
roron	live (n)
rotu	author
rotune	authority
roved	rather
ru	shine
rub	jump
rubri	card
rufer	erupt
rum	until
rut	root
rutuk	curtain
ruyava	excite

S

sabom	left (direction)
sado	saddle
saf	cap
safek	safe
satekwi	safety
safte	capture
safuz	secure
safuzune	security
sag	help
saga	heir
sagambri	hierarch
sagambriu	hierarchy
sagar	cradle

sahop	right (direction)	**sda**ki	drive
sajit	purse	sdal	sirens
saka	red	sdan	snake
sakij	athlete	sdas	expand
sakij**i**zim	athletic	sdas	spand
sama	look	**sde**di	prefer
samad	analyze	sde**dit**int	preference
saman	may	**sde**fe	pretend
sa**man**ev	maybe	sdegda	prepare
samoj	dinner	sdegda**Ħ**e	preparatory
samwa	nominee	sde**Ħoe**	sponsor
samwlj	nominate	**sde**jalj	demonstrate
sani	essay	**sde**li	blank
sans	sans	**sde**mirj	premier
sarip	script	sdem**le**po	clay
sasan	goose bump	**sde**mu	rush
sasda	stream	**sde**ne	steady
sat	salt	sdeneu	steady
satu	salty	sde**pe**bla	brave
Sa**tus**dum	Saturday	sde**pe**bla	courage
sawa	plan	sde**pev**mla	dictionary
sawan	plant	**sde**p**go**	lead
sayek	save	sde**pgoe**	leader
sazuj	there	sde**pgo**wi	leadership
sa**zuj**mar	therefore	**sde**plet	heart
sdafe	late	sdepletdu**me**ka	heartfelt
sdafoe	later	**sde**po	front
sda**Ħ**	spawn	sde**po**mot	before
sdaja	sky	sder	super
sda**jafa**Ħ	lightening	**sder**blir	supermarket
sdajlun	diamond	sdero**pe**o	terrify

sdewoe	boss
sdewoe	supervisor
sdiflun	serious
sdi**ga**go	mention
sdij	balance
sdiki	fact
sdikiƕe	factor
sdikiƕeu	factory
sdilo	style
sdis	hear
sdo	snow
sdona	bright
sdonix	snowball
sduan	premise
sduat	learn
sdume	day
sdumu	daily
sdunsi	sun
sdunsiu	sunny
sduruĦ	stretch
sdu**zi**ju	curious
sedo	none
sefer	set
sefermaki	setting
seƕi	process
selewi	property
selis	cell phone
seloe	prop
seloe	proper
sem	pack
semjag	package

senula	discover
seoko	globe
seo**ko**di	global
seo**nde**	around
sepaz	goodbye
sepaz	greeting
sepaz	hello
sepaz	peace
sepou	seventh
serad	close
serenune	serenity
seripi	discreet
serket	contain
serum	lady
sese	soft
siaĦa	civil
sifla	shop
siga	other
siga**ka**da	otherwise
sigda	has
sigda	have
sigda	possess
sika	cigar
si**ka**mle	cigarette
sike	must
si**ki**lan	listen
siki**ne**kev	audition
sikit	audio
si**ko**e	audience
sikuala	rip
sileble	mumble

silewa	silence	sisu	sixth
simaj	male	siti	city
sina	commune	sitioe	citizen
sinabaz	company	siu	squeeze
sinaizi	communist	sived	highway
sinapik	community	siwan	ascent
sinazim	communism	skabaz	spend
sinbex	comment	skajav	major
siney	computer	skajavune	majority
sinit	appear	skap	list
sinkonka	complain	skiwi	pick
sinlao	companion	sko	from
sinli	commit	skuHtu	scandal
sinlibex	commitment	slakun	triangle
sinlioe	committee	slan	scratch
sinmo	comfort	slas	fool
sinmoe	comforter	slati	pay
sinodi	commercial	slaxijag	average
sinplelj	complicate	sler	cheap
sinplex	complex	slili	elite
sinsem	compact	slu	down
sinum	compete	slu	low
sip	high	sluoe	lower
sip	up	slu-pleme	debacle
sipa	height	slutone	downtown
sipHemi	update	sma	style
siplad	upon	smanki	figure
sipobont	arrogant	smas	stare
sir	sear	smasdun	star
sisanda	semester	smeki	allow
sisdume	Sunday	smeki	let

smi	anger
smiu	angry
smup	gold
snapu	snappy
snir	sneer
snomu	tow
snuj	lie
soeHen	nature
sojwa	weapon
sok	cat
sok**gi**ab	catwalk
sokoe	soccer
so**sa**ngo	house
sota	stick
sot**au**	sticky
Spayn	Spain
spiln	spill
spim	job
spleyn	how
suaz	cross
sub	plight
suert	lemon
cucrt**ato**	lemonade
sufa	stuff
suliu	stealth
sumat	assume
sun	certain
sun	sure
sun**une**	certainty
supine	turn
surda**H**a	surprise

sur**o**nde	surround
surpey	surface
suv**en**in	souvenir
swa**kau**	envelop
swa**kau**	envelope
swey	put
swir	visit
sya	am
sya	is
sy**e**ka	was
sy**e**ka	were
syeki	psych
syekiu	psyche
syen	kind
syen	type
syenlj	organize
syenlj**ek**ev	organization
syenodi	typical
syokum	prove

T

ta	the
tabey	shy
tabey	timid
tahak	flat
tahakas	mattress
ta**H**omi	sacrifice
tale	value
tale**ti**em	invest
tale**ti**embex	investment
taletizoula	investigate

tale**tizou**lev	investigation
tama	wife
tamle	priority
tamya	pull
tamya	rank
tan	stand
tan	than
tana	status
tange	tax
tan**go**bet	platform
tat	that
taveḤ	lash
tavey	brow
ta**vi**mir	hair
ta**vu**jag	privilege
tavulj	private
ta**vu**mla	privacy
taxi	taxi
tazot	helicopter
tead	steady
tega	spot
tegimya	spotlight
telewuekev	television
tem	them
te**mi**rum	themselves
ten	then
tenez	tennis
tenix	mold (for copy)
Tenka	September
tenko	although
tenko	though
teris	theory
tey	they
tiem	when
tilme	spin
tine	charge
tinint	dominance
tis	this
Tiye	March
to	side
to**aba**	mold (fungus)
tobes	bunch
togar	neghbor
to**gar**sos	neighborhood
tok	suck
tokik	sidekick
tonaj	toes
tone	town
top**oe**	host
tos	those
tot	case
tradeke**vo**di	tradition
trajin	faith
tramlit	nerve
trani	fuse
trao	boast
trao	brag
trat	bend
treḤi	blind
tre**lua**	boost
trenu	ticket
treu	third

trevo	bore	**twil**itef	photograph
trevoeka	bored	twilitefoe	photographer
trinilj	celebrate	**twil**sir	camera
trinune	celebrity	twir	score
trofgobet	transform	twotlj	dedicate
trofgobetekev	transformation	**twu**vu	tough
trofyoekev	translation	**tya**ri	ready
trofyolf	translate	tyev	cable
tu**a**zib	choose		
tuazing	choice	**U**	
tuazum	volunteer	u**a**mu	conspicuous
tufa	grace	uamu	obvious
tumfte	suffer	uamu	palpable
tumftejag	suffrage	uan	eye
tunder	thunder	uawa	observe
tus	nice	ubam	count
tusava	polite	u**ba**memoe	calendar
tux	model	ubamoe	counter
twable	stumble	**ud**an	urban
twak	happen	ude	disk
twama	quiet	uf	roof
twane	badge	**u**fan	doubt
twango	vote	uH	level
twangoe	voter	uhev	connect
twapa	weight	uhev	mount
twar	secret	uhev	stem
tweni	shoot	u**hi**taka	need
twenjetaze	therapeutic	ujot	judge
twenjetizi	therapist	u**jot**bex	judgment
twen**je**tu	therapy	u**ka**zo	send
twili	photo	u**ka**zolj	delegate

ukonj	solve
ukonjekev	solution
ukua	equal
ukune	equality
ulan	charm
ulap	conjure
ulaz	pregnant
uleyu	imply
uleyulj	implicate
uli	with
ulin	among
uline	without
ulnelowi	nudity
ulrauoe	administer
ulseta	impress
ulsetaekev	impression
uma	woman
umadoe	manners
umar	armor
umle	Spring (season)
umon	would
une	call
unelo	naked
unipi	mouth
upi	depend
urj	urge
Urope	Europe
Uropi	European
uros	age
usij	south
usijaze	southern

uta	seal
utamaki	ceiling
utwaj	rent
uveli	along
uwabe	desert
uwodar	esteem
uya	mobile

V

vadni	group
vafa	float
vagHi	quit
valaH	submit
valekev	subsist
valHijwi	oblique
valpalit	subject
valtrima	science
valu	p.m.
valud	suburb
valudan	suburban
vamiont	frequent
vamiontmla	frequency
vanau	free
vanausos	freedom
vanila	vanilla
vasapu	issue
veato	victory
ved	way
vehask	trample
veHask	treat
venibex	environment

venibya	economy
venmaki	wedding
Vensdum	Wednesday
verna	winter
vi	very
vi	so
video	video
vigda	dirt
vigda	earth
vihuHyuj	distraught
vijir	silver
vik	practice
vikazeodi	practical
viki	spy
vip	fear
virgda	nose
visa	visa
vlun	lord
vo	it
vomirum	itself
von	chain
vuros	rage
vurpo	drag
vurpue	upset
vyu	sorry

W

wabe	narrative
wabe	saga
wabip	dynamic
wabo	blow
wadin	reluctant

wafe	correct
wafe	right
wafe	true
wafekev	correction
wafeu	truly
wafeu	truth
wagum	wallet
waka	fresh
walava	ignite
wan	direct
wanekev	direction
wanomi	veer
wari	tank
watrefe	righteous
watu	fifth
weblem	birth
weblemeka	born
weblem-sdume	birthday
wedej	strut
wedoj	social
wedune	society
wem	sad
wemeka	sadden
wey	swivel
widar	bar
wige	sick
wiski	whiskey
wist	twist
wist	wind (v)
woha	roar
wohi	throw

wone	cast		
wos**m**idu	teenage	x**e**tag	strap
wu	see	**x**far	die
wube	tub	**x**ine	expose
wubeta	bath	**x**ini	glass
wub**lou**	transparent	xix	camp
wu**e**ka	seen	xix**a**ne	campaign
wu**e**kev	envision	x**o**e	swagger
wu**e**kev	vision	x**o**mla	pen
wu**e**kevizim	optimism	**xo**vi	pencil
wuɧ	wind	x**pa**tr**i**at	expatriate
wu**ka**tij	documentary	x**u**mine	virtue
wula	door	x**u**minid	virtual
wulaklj	survey	x**u**ninidu	virtually
wula**ma**je	doorman	**Y**	
wum	seem	yabeta**flo**di	official
wuma**e**kev	option	ya**da**ta	bachelorette
wut	seek	ya**da**tin	bachelor
wu**toe**	agent	yale**ta**flo	office
X		ya**po**naze	establish
xa	military	ya**po**naze**be**x	establishment
xabo	box	**ya**smir	alone
xab**oe**s	boxers	**ya**su	by
xaji	sex	ya**su**jag	hostage
xa**jiu**	sexy	yat	sleep
xaka	exact	**y**awelj	crusade
xa**ka**u	exactly	ye	yes
xali	cost	**ye**ha	affirm
xali	expense	**ye**je	love
xali	price	yek	bare
xeka	term	ye**kle**vun	friend (plus)

yeku	barely	yogoe	expert
yelada	express	yogoe	maven
yelagau	liaison	yoin	media
yelao	join	yoket	know
yelo	partner	yoketumon	known
yelun	picture	yokiplindoe	newcomer
yem	place	yokipseran	newspaper
yeobex	pleasure	yol	kiss
yeoe	power	yolej	race
yeoel	powerful	yolejodi	racial
yepanj	coffee	yolejzim	racism
yepeko	jewelry	yoni	should
yepo	black	yoniln	feature
yepuli	plum	yuja	happy
yera	simple	yuk	brut
yerau	simply	yuk	bully
yet	nap	yukodi	brutal
yetra	strive	yum	deed
yevla	crime	yunan	nation
yeye	mother	yunanodi	national
yi	poor	yunanodiune	nationality
yibla	pour	yunini	baby
yikonka	explain	yups	yuppies

Z

yimey	gaze
yimlin	base
yin	say	za	migrate
yineka	said	zabi	cow
yiopa	please	zabiomaj	cowboy
yocup	planets	zabo	select
yof	dictate	zaboekev	selection
yofoe	dictator	zafe	okay

zaga	kill
zaga	murder
zahubri	difficult
zan	but
zan	however
zan**e**ka	special
zan**e**li	different
za**ne**nu	argue
za**ne**nubex	argument
zapi	dollar
zed	try
zed**o**di	trial
zegi	porno
ze**g**iyelun**a**ze	pornographic
zejup	dress (n)
ze**ma**zi	extraordinary
zeme	extra
zenk	oil
zensen	recent
zen**s**enu	recently
zey	polish
zi**a**fe	alright
zidaH	struggle
zigu	cry
ziHi	tear
ziki	bucket
zi**ki**sak	regimen
z**i**mko	affect

zimko**e**kev	affection
Zinga	November
zir	keep
zirva	store
zist	answer
ziw**i**o	design
ziw**i**oe	designer
zobraj	summer
zo**fi**vik	industry
zolum	bomb
zom	spread
zo**u**bla	vulnerable
zo**u**blaune	vulnerability
zo**u**la	open
zoulj	tolerate
zou**mau**	tolerant
zouti	blossom
zovu**rou**s	outrage
zow	hate
zowan	candid
zowanlj	candidate
zowanljune	candidacy
zugoklj	fascinate
zuHu	aggressive
zuHuwi	aggressiveness

Guide

Study tips

40 Phrases

Chapter One – Sepaz!

Chapter Two – Kojmede

Chapter Three – Pimeys

Chapter Four – Ni Ta Gdunuj

Practice Reading Passages

Answer Key

Study Tips

1. Make a commitment. You've already made a financial investment by purchasing these study materials, why not actually use them and get the most out of what you paid for?

2. Remember, if you don't use it you'll loose it. This is all the more reason to commit.

3. Practice at least 15 minutes a day – EVERYDAY. Don't be afraid, just do it. In the time that it may take to shower, you can be done with your lesson for the day. Always keep in mind that learning a new language requires consistent review and practice.

4. Read each section out loud. Don't be embarrassed about mispronouncing a word or stumbling over a phrase. Learning a language takes time and practice and will soon come fluidly with a good amount of effort.

5. Master the alphabet (and sounds). Pay special attention to the vowel sounds in the grammar section of the dictionary. The vowels are the key to correct pronunciation, but there are special sounds/ letter

combinations in this language that will require special attention as well.

6. Continue to review and refer back to the grammar section of the dictionary. In the exercises, important suffixes constantly pop up. Don't let them catch you off guard! The grammar section will assist you in these tricky spots.

7. Repeat each lesson until you understand it completely. The workbook section is designed to start off extremely easy and become progressively challenging. If you do not completely grasp the concepts of each exercise or activity you may find yourself stuck in a future exercise over the same concept. If you are not learning this language in a formal classroom setting, you have the luxury of studying the language at your own pace.

8. Pay attention to details. Fortunately there are no special accent symbols that hover over any of the letters to confuse you, but there are other rules to attend to, like never capitalizing the "h" unless you are meaning it to symbolize the "Ħ." Don't let the details trip you up.

9. Memorize the 40 phrases. Of course, you will be memorizing a lot more vocabulary, but if you at least have the 40 phrases under your belt, everything else may come much easier.

10. Practice reading the passages in the back of this section. Because there is limited literature written in the language, these passages should be very valuable to you.

11. Make flashcards to review throughout the day. Take a 3 x 5 index card and write a word on one side of the card in English and the translation on the other side in Hodaoa-Anibo. You might want to stash your flashcards in a convenient place to review for small available stretches of time, like on your lunch break, or while you're getting your oil changed.

12. Post labels or phrases in one room (or more). For example: using a 3 x 5 card (or even a scrap of paper will do), write down the word "window" in Anibo (kadabaz) and tape it to the window. Repeat for other items in the room. If you'd rather work on phrases, you can write them down instead and post them in strategic places, like over the light switch or on the door.

13. Find a partner to practice with. For now, it may be a challenge finding other Anibo speakers to buddy up with, but you can still use a non-Anibo speaker to help you in a variety of ways. For example, your partner can dictate a word to you from the dictionary, or a vocabulary list as you write it down in Anibo, testing your skills – which brings us to the next study tip…

14. Test yourself. Although you're working at your own pace, it's a good idea to test yourself to see where you are. This is where our partner and flashcards come in handy. Even if you don't have a partner, your flash cards may be enough by using time (speed) as a factor in testing.

15. Keep an Anibo journal. A journal is great to keep even when you have completed your lessons. A journal also provides you with instant Hodaoa-Anibo literature to read once you have mastered the pages in the back.

16. Use Anibo as a tool for meditation and/or relaxation. If you meditate by chanting mantras, consider translating them into Anibo. As a relaxation tool,

concentrate on deep breathing in a comfortable place and count to ten and then back down to one in Anibo repeatedly.

17. Teach someone else. It's amazing how much you retain when you are instructing someone else. It doesn't have to be all-out instruction, it could be as simple as a few vocabulary words and a few phrases. Although this new language could use all the teachers it can get, every little bit taught counts in a big way.

18. Don't give up! We all are very busy in our lives and our efforts can sometimes be derailed or distracted by interruptions in our schedule, emergencies and countless other reasons. If you have to put your lessons down for a minute, don't feel like all is lost. Just pick it back up again so that what you previously retained can help get you back on track. Also, while studying a language, sometimes you might feel like you are plateauing, but don't sabotage your efforts. The feeling of plateauing is a natural part of the learning process and if you start feeling like you're not learning anything, go back to the first lesson and look at how far you've progressed.

19. Enjoy your new language. There is more to a language than just words – there is a culture and a way of thinking. So many contributions can be made to the culture and the Anibo art and literature. Find your own way to contribute and make your stamp – your name apart of Hodaoa Anibo history.

40 Phases

1. Hello . . . Sepaz (pronounced –
   say.**pawz**)

2. Goodbye . . . Sepaz (pronounced –
   say.**pawz**)

3. Good morning . . . Giye manlu
   (pronounced - **gee**.yay **mawn**.loo)

4. Good afternoon . . . Giye nopau
   (pronounced – **gee**.yay **no**.pow)

5. Good night . . . Giye beslum
   (pronounced – **gee**.yay **bay**.sloom)

6. How are you . . . Balpu
   (pronounced – **bal**.poo)

7. I am fine . . . Balpa giye
   (pronounced – **bal**.pa **gee**.yay)

8. You look good . . . Pu sama giye
   (pronounced – poo **sah**.mah
   gee.yay)

9. Thank you . . . Gdasije pu
   (pronounced – gda.**see**.jay. poo)

10. I am tired . . . Pa sya broyeka
    (pronounced – pa syah broy. **ekah**)

11. I am hungry . . . Pa sya lavatu
    (pronounced – pa sya la**vah**.too)

12. Dinner is served . . . Samoj sya
    renj (pronounced - sa**moj**. sya.
    renj)

13. What time is it . . . Kimey ore sya
    vo (pronounced – **kee**.may oray sya
    voh)

14. It is time for you to get a watch . .
    .Vo sya emi mot pu ka dupun a fod
    (pronounced – vo sya. **emee**. mot
    poo ka doo**poon** a fod)

15. Would you like something to drink
    . . . Likamon pu dokapgo ka fua
    (pronounced - **lee**.kamohn poo
    dohk.**ap**go kah fwah)

16. What do you have? . . . Kimey
    Ħenix pu sigda (pronounced –
    keemay.shay**nix**.poo.**sig**da)

17. I don't understand . . . Pa Ħenix ne
    loirtan (pronounced – pa shay.**nix**
    nay loh.**eerton**)

18. Don't play silly . . . Ħenix ne gduhi
    slasaze (pronounced – shay.**nix** nay
    gdoo.hi slas.**az**.ay)

19. How was your day? . . . Splyen
    syeka ih'pu sdume (pronounced –
    splyayn **sye**.kah **ee**.poo **stoo**.may)

20. It was good . . . Vo syeka giye
    (pronounced – voh **sye**.kah
    gee.yay)

21. It was bad . . . Vo syeka badz
    (pronounced – voh **sye**.kah bahdz)

22. I feel sleepy . . . Pa dum yatu
    (pronounced – pa doom **yah**.too)

23. Are you okay? . . . Pu zafe
    (pronounced – poo **zah**.fay)

24. Yes, why? . . . Ye, gala (yay.
    gahla)

25. What are you doing? . . . Kimey pu
    Henixmaki (pronounced - **kee**.may
    poo shay.nix.**mah**.kee)

26. I'm doing my thing . . . Pa sya
    Ħenix ih'pa apgo. (pronounced –
    pa sya shay.**nix ee**.pa. **ap**.go)

27. Wake up . . . Gdusip (pronounced –
    gdoo.seep)

28. I am sorry . . . Pa sya vyu
    (pronounced – pah syah vyoo)

29. I forgive you . . . Pa motejma pu
    (pa. mo.**tej**.maa poo)

30. Who are you with? . . . Ken pu uli
    (pronounced - ken poo **oo**.lee)

31. I am with them . . . Pa sya uli tem
    (pronounced – pa sya **oo**.lee tem)

32. How do you feel? . . . Splyen pu
    dum (pronounced – splyen poo
    doom)

33. I feel great . . . Pa dum lefij
    (pronounced – pa doom lay.**feej**)

34. I'm about to go . . . Pa tyari ka mip
    (pronounced – pa **tyah**.ree ka
    meep)

35. Are you ready? . . . Pu tyari
    (pronounced – poo **tyah**.ree)

36. Get off of me . . . Dupun dibey pa
    (pronounced – doo.**poon dee**.bay
    pah)

37. You are funny . . . Pu plaꟾu
    (pronounced – poo **pla**.shoo)

38. I need that . . . Pa uhitaka tat
    (pronounced – pah oo.**hee**.tah.ka
    taht)

39. Bless you . . . Dej pu (pronounced
    – dej poo)

40. I love you . . . Pa yeje pu
    (pronounced – pa **yay**.jay poo)

Chapter One – Sura Pik Sepaz!

Greetings

- greetings – sepaz
- hello – sepaz
- goodbye – sepaz
- good – giye
- morning – manlu
- afternoon – nopau
- evening - beslum
- How are you? – Balpu?
- I'm fine. – Balpa giye.

Exercise I (Labin pik)

In the following exercise, look at the times listed. Besides each time, give the appropriate greeting on the provided line in Ħodaoa-Anibo. Choose between: Good morning (Giye manlu); Good afternoon (Giye nopau); and Good night (Giye beslum).

Example (roaba):

8:00 a.m. = Giye manlu

1. 4:30 p.m.   _____

    _____   _____

    _____
                                  5. 12:30
2. 9:15 a.m.   p.m.

    _____   _____

    _____   _____

3. 11:20   6. 12:17
    a.m.   a.m.

    _____   _____

    _____   _____

4. 11:20
    p.m.

Dialog 1 (Magezi pik)

Amari: Giye manlu kipo.

Rashaun: Giye manlu kipo. Balpu?

Amari: Balpa giye. Gdasije pu mot palmaki.
Li balpu?

Rashaun: Pa dum yatu.

Amari: Pu uhitaka ka gdubsip!

Exercise II (Labin dit)

Tell what time of day the following
activities are done: *manlu*, *nopau*, or
beslum. There will be multiple possibilities
for some answers.

1. Eat breakfast

   _____

2. Wake up

    _____

3. Shower

    _____

4. Leave for work

    _____

5. Leave for elementary school

    _____

6. Eat dinner

    _____

7. Eat lunch

    _____

8. Run weekend errands

    _____

Family

- aunt (m) – yeomba
- aunt (p) – Hangazi
- brother – kipo
- cousin – etaki
- daughter – jeki
- family – ajega
- family friend (man) – ahi
- family friend (woman) – aki
- father – bati
- grandma – kujayeye (or kujaye)
- grandpa – kujabati (or kujaba)
- husband - nabsu
- mother – yeye
- nephew (brother) – majipo
- nephew (sister) – kemin
- niece (brother) – majom
- niece (sister) – komba
- sister – keki
- son – jevat
- uncle (m) – yami
- uncle (p) – gdogo
- wife – tama/ onabu

Exercise III (Labin tre)

In the following exercise, lists of relationships are
stated. Beside each relationship in English, write the
simplified version of the relationship in Hodaoa-
Anibo in a complete sentence. Remember, the
possession rule using " ih'."

Example: *The woman who gave birth to*
                you...
                Tis sya ih'pa yeye. (This is my
                mother.)

1.   Your mother's son...

     _____

2.   Your sister's daughter...

     _____

3.   Your father's daughter ...

     _____

4.   Your brother's son...

     _____

5.   Your mother's mother...

     _____

6.   Your father's mother...

     _____

7.   Your father's sister ...

     _____

8.   Your father's brother...

     _____

9.   Your female
     offspring..._____

Dialog II (Magezi dit)

Bea: Pa sya ih'Deondre yeye!

Fatimah: Pa yoket. Pa sya ih'eney yeomba!

Bea: Deondre yoni zoula ih'pa ejimi ozuja!

Fatima: Erem sya ih'pu nabsu?

Bea: No! Henix ne nub ka eney - eney sya maoved ladit ih'pu to!

Exercise IV (Labin kad)

In the following exercise, read the English questions about your family carefully and respond to each question in Hodaoa-Anibo using complete sentences.

Example: *What is your brother's name?*
                Ih'pa ih'kipo nama Marques.

1.   What is your mother's name?

_____

2.   What is your father's name?

_____

3.   How many sisters do you have?

_____

4.   What is your brother's son's name?

_____

5.   What is your grandmother's sister to you?

_____

6.   How old is your grandfather?

_____

7.   Who, in your family, has influenced you
     most?

_____

8.   Who, in your family, gives the best gifts?

_____

9. Who, in your family, borrows the most
    money?

    _____

10. Who, in your family, is the organizer of
    most family events?

    _____

11. Who, in your family, is the most talented?

    _____

12. Who, in your family, has the most children?

    _____

Activity I (Rakapudau pik)

Read the following poem aloud as fast as possible without making mistakes. Each time you stumble start from the beginning until you can say the entire poem fluidly.

Reconat

Pa ejma umon mapgo

Ka twama ta dibela

FerHmaki ta egimaki kerpo

Tat pedonj ih'jas yeje ka duleka

Ih'pa kenin neok ka ta bipo

Bari a xini eli bari lawa

Umaj ne lika bati nefa kipo

Ih'pa rakekev ih'pa sojwa

Pik sdume pu motejmaumo pa

Li samanev motopun ih'pa pabo

Zan neHi ta jagda

Nemotopunbla wabo

Chapter Two - Sura Dit

Kojmede

Food

- apple - pum
- banana – banaya
- bread – mofla
- cake – makate
- cheese – jibini
- celery – pio
- cherry – reĦa
- cookie – fula
- fish – nag
- grapefruit – refuit
- lemon – suert
- milk – maĦ
- milkshake – maĦjote
- orange – ronjiwa
- pepper – epli
- vanilla – vanila
- chicken – mlanile
- beef – noyan
- pork - ruwe
- eggs – bai
- sugar – suka
- grape – sapibu
- rice – wali
- broccoli – preko
- spinach – midwere
- potato – jeupe
- corn – suguru
- pancakes – miati
- chocolate – Ħokola
- almond – lamoz
- ice cream – raf tyendi
- eat – koron
- drink – fua

Exercise I (Labin pik)

Below is a recipe in Ħodaoa-Anibo. Read the recipe and answer the questions that follow in English in complete sentences.

Banaya Lamoz MaĦjote

Pu uhitakaumo:
- Pik kombe bari hrep banayas
- Pik kombe bari raf
- Dit kombes bari vanilla raf tyendi
- Pik kombe bari lamoz maĦ
- Pik mlanoe

Wanekevs:

Swey maoe bari ta niatokev nika ta mlanoe li mlan mot gdefda pik ka ditfeys fa rum ta atofte sya kisayont.

1. Splyen fama banayas pu uhitaka?

_____

2. Kimey pu uhitaka ka mlan ta niatokevs?

_____

3. Tis dokapgo ka koron fa fua?

_____

4. Splyen fama raf pu uhitaka?

_____

5. Kimey syen bari maĦ pu uhitaka?

_____

6. Splyen fama bari tis maĦ pu uhitaka?

_____

7. Kimey syen bari raf tyendi pu uhitaka?

_____

8. Splyen fama raf tyendi Ħenix pu uhitaka?

_____

9. Splyen nuir pu mlan tis fua?

_____

10. Kimey sya ta nama bari tis fua?

_____

11. Kimey syen bari fua sya vo?

_____

12. Sya tis mlaba fa hubi ka klu?

_____

Dialog III (Magezi tre)

Lauren: Pa sya vi lavatu!

Hateem: Zan pu koroneka mawey!

Lauren: Vi kimey! Pa sya hiki lavatu.

Tanj: Pa sigda a banaya. Pu kamoe vo?

Lauren: No, pa Ħenix ne lika banayas.

Tanj: Ten pu sike ne ekev tal lavatu!

Hateem: Pa sigda Ħokola.

Lauren: Ra pa sigda dok?

Exercise II (Labin dit)

The following are a series of math problems. Solve the equations and write the answers on the lines provided in Ħodaoa-Anibo in complete sentences.

1. Ix pa sigda dit pums, lip u sigda wat pums. Splyen fabaz Ħenix jas sigda ni maoe?

_____

2. Ix pa sigdaeka okaĦ aka makates lip u koroneka deje dit bari tem, splyen fabaz sigdumo pa milineka?

_____

3. Ix pu sigdaeka trewo bais li pa sigdaeka deje wat bais, li Amari sigdaeka sepowo bais, splyen fabaz bais pu li Amari sidaumon makau?

_____

4. Uli pik reĦa; sis suerts; deje ronjiwas; deje pik sapibus; kadwo pums; li none refuits, splyen fabaz dipos bari fuit nikama?

_____

Riddles I (Ribix pik)

1. Erem sya ta leji ta liamu?

2. Splyen fabaz nopas evuꞪ pik li piꞪ aka?

3. Splyen fabaz fulas ra pu koron ladit a amtip kyogis?

4. Erem sya ta anba yem ta wu a maje-koronmaki nag?

5. Imos sya wafe: nopa li wat sya deje-tre fa nopa li wat syeka deje-tre?

6. Kimey Ɦenixeka pik amajukint jele yin ka ta siga amajukint jele?

7. Kimey Ɦenixeka ta Ɦokola wider yin ka ta lalipop?

8. Kimey mip sip zan neꞪi relin slu?

9. Kimey Ɦenixeka Washington evrelin bulamot ih'eney dejeu* amemo? (keep the "-th" rule for numbers in mind)

10. Erem apgos mip ritra, kimey ra pu maoved ubam ladit?

Chapter Three – Sura Tre

Pimeys

Colors

black – yepo	red – saka
brown – boron	yellow – karo
burgundy – mogdul	white – jux
blue – luk	gold – smup
green – munje	silver – vijir
grey – guay	lavender – fubrau
purple – zambrau	orange (color) – ronj
	pink – fusak

Exercise I (Labin pik)

Circle the colors within each of the following sentences. Then find each of the colors found in the sentences in the word search puzzle.

1. Pa pini beraeka a fusak esoroes.

2. Sazuj syeka ne yepo majes gazu.

3. Eney genu kuvip vijir ne smup.

4. Pa yeje ih'eney boron uans

5. Enin pabo syeka saka

6. Sazuj sya neapgo lika luk sdajas li munje jani.

7. Ih'pa ronjiwa sya ronj.

8. hapimey ta gabeys jux.

9. Henix ne ekev rodingeka bari a guay klo.

10. Pa ratun karo kavihis sya mot gakup ken sya lavatu mot ahudekev.

11. Fod nine mot ta baigmaki zambrau gakup koronoe.

12. Ih'Fatimah giniba pimey sya fubrau.

Word Search

```
Z  A  M  B  R  A  U  S  T  U
I  B  O  R  O  N  B  A  D  E
R  F  G  H  R  L  U  K  J  E
G  K  A  R  O  K  L  A  M  J
N  U  O  P  N  F  Y  R  S  N
Z  I  A  F  J  U  X  E  X  U
T  U  V  Y  W  S  M  U  P  M
Y  F  U  B  R  A  U  Z  A  O
V  I  J  I  R  K  A  R  O  B
```

Dialog IV (Magezi kad)

Shaunte: Hey ojuma! Pa lika tos saka fubs!

Fatimah: Dindu? Pu Ħenix ne ratun tat tey sya rix fama mot labo?

Shaunte: Oh ne ojuma! Tey sya vi
mleℏuni.

Fatimah: Pa pini dupuneka tem tis jutazo,
uli dok karo, jux, yepo li boron piks pini lika
tem.

Shaunte: Erem ℏenixeka pu dupun tem?

Fatimah: Tat sya ih'pa twar.

Exercise II (Labin dit)

Listed below are pairs of colors in ℏodaoa-
Anibo. Beside each pair, write (in Anibo)
the color each pair would make if the colors
were mixed.

    1.   Saka li karo

         _____

    2.   jux li yepo

         _____

    3.   luk li saka

         _____

    4.   fusak li karo

         _____

    5.   karo li luk

         _____

6. zambrau li jux

   _____

7. jux li saka

   _____

8. munje li karo

   _____

Activity I (Rakapudau pik)

Read the following poem and create a song using your own melody. Sing your song out loud three times, and go as slow or as quickly as you feel is necessary.

Ħenix Ne Ekev Rodingeka

Ħenix ne ekev rodingeka bari ta adi bari ta wuĦ

Kimimaki blos ta kadabaz nit a gdunuj

Jotemaki maoe ta rutuk li wulas

Wabomaki vigda patrins li gawar povoda

Pa umo zir pu safek

Pu umo ne wabo aved

Pini lika azyejiz Ħenix

Ta wuĦ pini kamoe ka gduhi

Translation (Trofyoekev)

Translate the following paragraph into
Hodaoa-Anibo.

One father of two daughters by two different
mothers said, "The mother of my other
daughter, she expects the same. If I tell my
daughter I'm going to pick her up at 8 in the
morning, then no matter how tired I am I
better be there at 8. Not 9. Not 8:05..."
Friendly relationships encourage fathers to
maintain consistent contact.

_____

_____

_____

_____

_____

_____

_____

Chapter IV – Sura kad
Ni ta gdunuj

Kitchen

counter – ubamoe

sink – neok

tile – fyo

cabinet – hifek

refrigerator – frijoljoe

oven – etaf

stove – mlati

cook – mlaga

dish – bese

plate – dakome

spoon – tiji

fork – randi

knife – sdesu

bowl – aku

blender – mlanoe

burn – mogda

stir – siHa

fire – ajote

pilot – bloten

microwave – myurusa

spatula – tapinoe

ladle – pepipoe

towel – bey

saucer – mleyn

cup (mug) – dusi

glass – xını

pot – huel

pan – bahuel

kitchen – gdunuj

Exercise I (Labin pik)

Complete the following sentences with words that would
make sense from the vocabulary box. Rewrite the sentences
on the lines provided in English.

neok   bloten

    myurusa   ajote   siHa

    xini   bey

1. Pu ra febin ta beses ni ta _____.

_____.

2. Ekev sun ne ta axe ta _____.

_____.

3. Yiopa flejot ih'eney kojmede ni ta _____.

_____.

4. Henix ne motupun ta _____vo sip tiem pu
    moveHi vo nine.

_____.

5. Supine ta _____slu.

_____.

6. Ekev brakel, ta _____Ħenix ne imya.

_____.

7. Oney ih'pu jenus li linj tem uli a _____.

_____.

Dialog V (Magezi wat)

Bea: Jevat, Ħenix pu yoket splyen ka mlaga?

Deondre: Pu sdiflun? Pa sya ta anba mlaga ni ta faye evto pu yeye!

Bea: Sya tat wafe?

Deondre: Tat sya wafe! Fod! Pa bujaumo pu kabeslum, li pu wumo.

Bea: Bi pa ra ne giwa. Ih'pa jevat mipmaki ka mlaga mot ih'eney yeye. Sya ne tat dokapgo?

Exercise II (Labin dit)

Fill in the blanks using the words from the vocabulary box. Write all answer in Ħodaoa-Anibo. Read the completed sentences out loud.

Tiji	aku		randi		sdesu
xinis	aku	bahuel		kombe	
	myurusa		mlati		etaf

1. Pa klueka a huel bari oatmeal li koronumo vo nine

   a _____ uli a _____.

2. Pa mlaga miatis ni a _____ ladit dyaki a

   _____.

3. Pa flejot sip kojmede nit a _____ fat a

   _____.

4. Pa fua nine bari a _____ evpedonj pa sya

   rodingeka ih'pa _____ akeumo.

5. Ħrep ta noyan uli a _____ li _____.

Activity III (Rakapudau tre)

Read the words in Ħodaoa-Anibo and on the spaces
provided, write down what the word(s) remind you of, or
sound like to you in English.

1. munje   _____
2. ajote   _____
3. aku   _____
4. sdesu   _____
5. dakome   _____
6. mlati   _____
7. Ħifek   _____
8. boron   _____
9. luk   _____
10. vIʝir   _____

Riddles II (Ribix dit)

1. Ra bunas sigda yuninis?

2. Kimey Ħenixeka ta oya yin ka ta paman?

3. Tiem Ħenix sdovus sigda oka pamans?

4. Kimey sigda piĦaka nues zan rane giab?

5. Kimey sya ta zanelint evuĦ a rokip peni li a fanin robo?

6. Ix pu ra bera oka beses mot ditwo-sis akats, splyen fabaz ra pu bera mot a akat li a robo?

7. Gala syeka ta opib aludljeka?

8. Kimey syen bari soda side pun ne fua?

9. Splyen Ħenix yeye Art nag?

10. Kimey Ħuba rap u baze bem sko ka pepoa a Ħofluj tat sya none?

Practice Reading Passages

Cloudy Less

I don't see grey clouds
I see nothing but white sky
No hint of sunshine

No hint of sunshine
A cool break from searing days
Calm for healing skin

Calm for healing skin
Is only temporary
Once white skies burn off

Klou Bazne

Pa Ħenix ne wu guay klos
Pa wıı neapgo zan jux sdaja
Ne hent bari sdunsi ru

Ne hent bari sdunsi ru
A kul axe sko sirmaki sdumes
Paz mot ferĦmaki eblin

Pax mot ferĦmaki eblin
Sya genu hunfaĦe
PiĦki jux sdajas mogda dibey

Thought

I thought of you love
Warm smile cold heart
I shiver
Still longing for you

Gokevinum

Pa ratuneka bari pu yeje
Flejot heki okꜦ sdeplet pa joteka
Hiki nuirmaki mot pu

Comfort

Wanting to relax
In the cradle of your heart
Looking out at things

Sinmo

Kamoemaki ka Ħona
Ni ta sagar bari ih'pu sdeplet
Samamaki nine an apgos

Gregory Hines

Growing up learning about the Nicholas Brothers, Sammy Davis, Jr., and watching a little kid like Savion Glover dance with a big name like Gregory Hines was quite inspiring to a little aspiring entertainer like myself. But because Hines has been taking tap lessons since he was a toddler, the man was in a different league. Hines once told the Associated Press, "When I realized I was alive and these were my parents, and I could walk and talk, I could dance."

Gregory Hines

Badarmaki sip sduatmaki gdefda ta Nikolas Kipos, Sammy Davis, Jr., li fodmaki a mle azyej lika Savion Glover bajun uli a faHabaz nama lika Gregory Hines syeka jumla enimusemaki ka a mle kamomaki nitopaoe lika ih'pa mirum. Zan evpedonj Hines ekeveka moveHmaki tap aznis huti eney syeka a afanu omaj, ta maje syeka ni a zaneli kunup. Hines piHki nudueka ta Kawedljeka LaHiseta, "Tiem pa dindljeka pa syeka karoron li His syeka ih'pa koganisiz, li pa muyaye giab li nub, pa muyaye bajun.

Answer Key

Chapter 1

Exercise 1

1. Giye nopau   2. Giye manlu   3. Giye manlu   4. Giye beslum   5. Giye nopau   6. Giye manlu

Exercise 2

1. manlu   2. answers will vary   3. answers will vary   4. answers will vary   5. manlu   6. beslum   7. nopau   8. manlu

Exercise 3

1. Tis sya ih'pa kipo.   2. Tis sya ih'pa komba.   3. Tis sya ih'pa keki.   4. Tis sya ih'pa majipo.   5. Tis sya ih'pa kujaye (or kujayeye).   6. Tis sya ih'pa kujaye (or kujayeye). 7. Tis sya ih'pa Ħagazi   8. Tis sya ih'pa gdogo.   9. Tis sya ih'pa jeki.

Exercise 4

All answers will vary.

Chapter 2

Exercise I (sentences may vary slightly)

1. I need one cup of bananas. 2. I need a blender.   3. This is something to drink.   4. I need one cup of ice.   5. I need almond milk.   6. I need one cup of almond milk.   7. I need vanilla ice cream.   8. I need two cups of vanilla ice cream.   9. I blend it for one to two minutes.   10. The name of this drink is: Banana

Almond Milkshake. 11. This is a milkshake. 12. This is easy to make.

Exercise 2

1.   Jas sigda sepo pums. 2. Pu sigdaumo sepoH aka okawo aka milineka. 3. Jas sigdaumon piH aka bais. 4. Sazuj sya siswo oka nikama.

Riddles I

1. ladit ta bipo. 2. ditwo 3. genu pik 4. ni a leji-kome koronis 5. neriH, nopa li wat sya deje kad 6. Wow, pa sigda herdons 7. Sepaz, tokoe! 8. ih'pu uros 9.deje pik 10. ih'pu honajiz

Chapter 3

Exercise I

1. fusak 2. yepo 3. vijir/smup 4. boron 5. saka 6. luk/munje 7. ronj 8. jux 9. guay 10. karo 11. zambrau 12. fubrau

Exercise 2

1. ronj 2. guay 3. zambrau 4. ronj 5. munje 6. fubrau 7. fusak 8. munje

Chapter 4

Exercise 1

1. neok 2. xinis 3. myurusa 4. siHa 5. ajote 6. bloten 7. bey

Exercise 2

1. aku/ tiji   2. bauel/ mlati   3. etaf/ myurusa   4. kombe/ xinis
5. sdesu/ randi

Riddles II

1. Ne, tey ra genu sigda bunas   2. Pu sya sweymaki pa ladit!
3. Tim sazuj sya dit bari tem   4. Watwo ditanas barijajis   5.
Ditwo kad akats   6. Oka   7. Mot aznumaki sip ta jajis   8.
Etagamaki soda   9. Uli askanij li usij ejnos   10. Ta Ħuba oka
– klueka sip bari dit nones, pik ladit dyaki bari ta siga

Notes

www.ingramcontent.com/pod-product-compliance
Lightning Source LLC
Chambersburg PA
CBHW020937090426
42736CB00010B/1170